GEOFF CHAPPLE
THE STORY BEHIND THE LEGEND

GEOFF CHAPPLE

THE STORY BEHIND THE LEGEND

CLIVE YOULTON

Front cover illustration courtesy of Garry Letts.

First published 2006

Stadia is an imprint of
Tempus Publishing Limited
The Mill, Brimscombe Port,
Stroud, Gloucestershire, GL5 2QG
www.tempus-publishing.com

British Library Cataloguing in Publication Data.
A catalogue record for this book is available from the British Library.

ISBN 0 7524 3800 X

Typesetting and origination by Tempus Publishing Limited
Printed in Great Britain

Contents

Acknowledgements

I would like to thank the following people for their help in making this book possible:

Firstly thanks to Holly Bennion and James Howarth at Tempus Publishing for taking on the concept I put to them in June 2005 and agreeing to publish it.

To my wife Nicki for her patience when all I have had on my mind for the past nine months is the next stage of this project.

To Geoff Chapple, for saying 'yes' when I asked if he would allow me the honour of writing his biography.

To all the people who have contributed by way of quotes for the book, in particular Colin Lippiatt for giving me his time and for providing me with his side of the story as far as his former boss is concerned.

To Justine Stevenson, for all her invaluable input in reading and editing my work, particularly in the few weeks leading up to the deadline.

To Tony Williams.

My thanks also go to those who have contributed images for the book; they are credited, where possible, in the picture captions.

Finally thank you to Sir Alex Ferguson for agreeing to write the Foreword and, last but not least, to Mark Doyle, who kindly provided a list of Geoff's achievements which form the final part of the book.

Author Clive Youlton

About the Author

Clive Youlton was born in 1962 in Guildford, Surrey. A talented sportsman, his passion was football and, having played at district and county representative level throughout his youth, his non-League career took in spells at Addlestone & Weybridge Town, Woking (twice) and Leatherhead. He made his senior debut for Addlestone aged seventeen, while he played as a regular for the club in the inaugural Southern League premier division as an eighteen-year-old. At Woking he was a striker during Geoff Chapple's first full season in charge and scored 31 goals in a total of 57 first team appearances for the Cards.

In 1993, aged thirty, he won the New Zealand National League's Golden Boot award, scoring 26 goals in 25 league games for Wanganui Athletic, a feat that earned him a mention in *World Soccer* magazine. That season he was one of four ever-presents in a side which also included former Woking stars Lloyd and Shane Wye. His goal tally equalled the record in a season at the top level of New Zealand soccer since records began in 1983. And he received one of four merit awards in the Wanganui Sportsperson of the Year competition; the first footballer in the town to be recognised in such a way.

Having become a sports journalist in 1998, as sports editor of the *Woking News and Mail* he has been commended in the Guardian Media Awards for Best Sports Writer and Best Sports Pages. In 2003 he became a published author for the first time, co-writing *Cards on the Table – Woking's Conference Years*.

Clive is married to Nicki and has two young children.

Geoff with Sir Alex Ferguson

Foreword

by Sir Alex Ferguson CBE

Geoff Chapple has a remarkable record of achievements in non-League football, which future generations of managers will find extremely difficult to emulate. Knowing what it is like to win at Wembley Stadium I think Geoff's record of five FA Trophy wins there in seven years was an incredible feat which, quite honestly, is likely to stand the test of time.

I have met Geoff on occasion and anybody who does so can't fail to be touched by his jovial personality and his passion for football which shines through. As someone who had that same feeling for the game instilled in me at a young age, I can only admire his dedication.

The fact this book has been written says everything about his accomplishments in football and just how high profile he became at Woking and then Kingstonian. It is an excellent account by Clive Youlton of his life and one which I'm sure will be enjoyed by all who read it.

Sir Alex Ferguson CBE

Introduction

There's something rather surreal about sitting in Geoff Chapple's dining room conducting an interview in the heat of mid-summer when he is urging me to swat as many daddy-long-legs as possible, while directing operations from the other side of the table. "Missed again – bit like your shooting," he'd chuckle through the haze of his cigarette smoke, referring to my days as a centre forward in his Woking team, as my attempted swipe only ends up disturbing fresh air.

Not just the one interview either, quite a few in fact since the day back in June 2005 when I approached him and asked whether he would agree for me to write his biography. I had already asked Tempus Publishing of course. And having got a positive response from James Howarth and Holly Bennion at the company I was relieved when Geoff said 'yes' to me, even though he had turned down other requests to carry out the daunting task.

Tracking him down of an evening has been the interesting part. His job as a courier meant I never knew until about an hour beforehand whether I was seeing him for our scheduled meeting or not. One night I got to his house at 7.30p.m. and he informed me he had to go to Ipswich to do a drop off once I'd finished with him. I felt guilty leaving two hours later knowing I would soon be in bed while he would be charging up to Suffolk. I found out the next day he got home at 4.30a.m.

I must say working on this book has been an adventure, which started with my phone call to Geoff and was followed by our first meeting in a coffee shop in Farnham, his home town and a place that has featured heavily in his life. Just like so many other meetings we had, that first one was comical. We ordered a sandwich and coffee, sat outside, and with me poised to deliver the opening gambit and let him know my proposals, he informed me he had lost his glasses, couldn't see anything without them and that he'd have to go and look for them. So there I was with two plates of sandwiches and two cups of coffee while Geoff retraced his steps back to the car park to look for the missing glasses. He returned twenty minutes later perspiring lightly and a little more red in the face than usual – and without them. They had dropped out of his pocket on the 200-yard walk from the car to the coffee shop, never to be seen again.

I have to be honest and say a book about him should have been written long before now, but seeing some of the ex-professional players who have put pen to paper in recent times, Geoff's story is hardly past its sell-by date. Trying to get hold of ex-managers and players has proved easier than I thought in some respects but tracking down everybody I would have liked to speak to was not possible for various reasons, not least the time element. Being given nine months to write a book of such magnitude was quite an ask; Geoff being a big subject in every sense of the word. Thankfully, with the invaluable help of my editing friend Justine Stevenson, I managed it, even though I now have to reacquaint myself with my wife Nicki and replace the cushion on which I've sat night after night, while working on my computer. Frankly it's worn out and having now passed my forty-third birthday, I know how it feels.

I must say it's been fun catching up with a lot of people I haven't spoken to for a long time in pursuit of those all-important quotes. When you've got two young children, life becomes centred on your family and it's easy to lose touch. Speaking to a chap named Adrian Corbett – I'd actually phoned to speak to his wife Lynn – was amusing in that when I told him who I was, he said to me "I used to pay to watch you play, can I have my money back?" I think he said it in jest but then you never know! As expected, I wasn't able to get former Woking goalkeeper Laurence Batty off the phone once I'd contacted him, but I enjoyed every minute of our chat. Of course I made the mistake of reminding him of the two best saves I ever saw him make and that they were both in the same game. "I know, I know," he volunteered. "Rushden away." Cue fifteen minutes of talking about the 'Batty years'. The passion of the likes of George Borg, Graham Allner, Paul Fairclough and John Still shone through and getting a variety of different angles from various sources was an enjoyable, if tiring, task. Meeting Colin Lippiatt for a drink and a chat in a Brewers Fayre in Bagshot was another entertaining evening, the highlight of which was when a waitress came to our table carrying two plates of food asking whether we'd ordered them. "Oh dear I can't find the people anywhere," she uttered, as we told her they weren't ours. "They're not out in the car park are they?" offered Colin, with one of those laughs that is appreciated fondly by anyone who knows him. For those I didn't get to contact, despite having every intention to do so, I apologise but time constraints and not being able to go beyond the allocated word count restricted me.

I hope it is a worthwhile read for all those who knew or worked with Geoff over the years – as well as for interested fans of the non-League game who didn't. It was never intended to be a series of sensational revelations, more a reflection of Geoff's life from his own recollections interspersed with quotes from key people. Some of those quotes are less than complementary as it would be impossible to go through twenty-five years as a football manager without upsetting one or two along the way. But it makes for a more rounded account and ultimately it is a better read because of it. I hope I have done it justice, as a book about Geoff Chapple deserves to be a good one, given his reputation in the game.

Clive Youlton
April 2006

1

Driving Down
Memory Lane

'I think we agree, the past is over' – George W. Bush

It was Stratton Street, central London, June 2003. A courier had arrived at his port of call, an office block at Stratton House, and was standing outside the building at the bottom of some steps preparing to deliver half a dozen parcels. He heaved them into his arms and, aware the lift was out of order, made his way up the stairs cursing and swearing along the way before emerging on the fourth floor out of breath, perspiring heavily and, in his words, absolutely knackered. Having made the drop he then staggered down the stairs again and emerged into the street. "Then I literally bumped into this bloke with a briefcase," says Geoff Chapple. "And his quote to me was 'bugger me, I knew you when you never had a belly'." The man with a memory for faces was Ken Bates, and it is a sign of the esteem in which the game of football held Chapple – now delivering parcels for a living – that the former Chelsea chairman, and now Leeds United chief, should act as though he had encountered a long lost friend. "It was around the time that Roman Abramovich had come in to take over Chelsea and I think Ken was heading to the Ritz, which was just over the road, to chat with him," Chapple adds. Meetings between Abramovich and Bates – whether or not the former Woking and Kingstonian boss was exact about the timing – were taking place without a doubt. And when the Russian oil baron finally put pen to paper at Stamford Bridge it became a defining moment for English football, given the millions of pounds he has since thrown at the west London club.

Chapple, the self-employed courier, once voted non-League manager of the era in the late 1990s, had already had his defining moment. It had come on 14 October 2002, a day which marked the end of his time in the spotlight as he was sacked as manager of his cherished Woking Football Club. The dismissal hit him hard. Such events in life can occur in an instant. Given the nature of football, with the success at all costs and damn the consequences culture, football managers are extremely susceptible to the unexpected becoming a reality. But a fortune-teller's skills would not in any way have been tested in foreseeing Chapple's sacking, given the disastrous run of results Woking had endured under his latest stewardship. It was to be Chapple's second and final exit from a club that had become emblazoned on his heart. Having been shown the door at Woking in particular and Conference football in general, he was at a big crossroads in his life.

As it turned out he managed to set himself up as a courier with the help of Matt Crossley, the former Wycombe Wanderers centre half who had become Chapple's captain at Kingstonian Football Club. Crossley, who was able to point Chapple in the right direction along the path to his new career, had first met Chapple in the car park of Wycombe's Causeway Stadium, then named Adams Park, back in 1997. Being in the process of stepping back from full-time football at that time because of a back problem, Crossley had an initial chat with Chapple before the meeting progressed into something more significant. "I had spoken to a lot of managers before that and they'd said 'give us a bell if you're not doing anything' and with Geoff, it was one of those conversations," says Crossley.

Chapple already had it in his mind to take Crossley to Woking in that summer of 1997, until his dramatic switch to Kingstonian at the last moment changed everything. "Actually it was Chris Kelly who rang me from Kingstonian and told me a top manager was going to the club and that I'd been earmarked by him to go there," adds Crossley. "I had a feeling it would be Geoff and did my homework before finding out that's who it was. I was already going to ring him about the possibility of going to Woking. The day I went down to Kingstonian to meet him I didn't have to go away and think about it. I signed straight away for Geoff because I liked what I heard and always liked the way his teams played. I also knew he would get a good team together and we'd have a good chance of winning the Ryman League. I was the first I think and then people like Gary Patterson and big Terry Evans came along. We had some great players in that team and we all had a bit of experience.

Geoff used to let us go out there and express ourselves. It took a couple of months to get it going but when it did we were a good side. I was proud to be his captain and I had a lot of respect for him, as did a lot of people at every level of the English game. Our friendship goes back a long way."

That allegiance was the basis on which Crossley helped Chapple get his feet under the table in the courier world. "I had a friend who owned a courier company and I got Geoff involved there," he says. "He hasn't got the pressure of the football and I think he's enjoying it." Chapple adds: "I didn't want to go back into financial consultancy [his first career]. If I did it would have meant retaking exams because the law keeps changing. I didn't want to do that at my time of life. And I couldn't imagine managing anyone else other than Woking. In any case I didn't have offers because I never put myself about and never went to football matches. I was out of the public eye."

Some managers apply for anything that moves in the job market but Chapple can't understand that mentality. "It doesn't add up really. It's about personal friendships. I've never been a creep at any time in my life. I don't ask people for anything." Chapple let the dust settle for a month after leaving Woking before taking on the opportunity offered him by Crossley. The company recommended to Chapple was Post Haste in Basingstoke. He wasn't scared of hard work and he had driven the country scouring talent as a football manager. Now he put the deposit down on a van and decided to get on with the next step in his life. "It was a bit of a culture shock really when I started," he says. "I deliver anything and I racked up 200,000 miles in the first two years. The first Christmas Day in the job, I left home at 5.30 in the morning and went straight through to 11p.m. When I got home I was just getting a bowl of soup when the phone rang. It was another job, so I was off again. I picked up from Odiham and went to Glasgow. That's when I'm thinking, 'what the hell am I doing?'."

While he never did any running around in the literal senses as a football manager, he does plenty these days, even though it's not on foot but in his Peugeot Partner van. He has been known to leave home at 2a.m. on his way to a far-flung northern outpost. But on a normal day he arrives at the depot at 7.30a.m. – having been on twenty-four-hour call – where he waits with a group of other drivers for his instructions for the day. "There'll be a couple of us already in before the boss arrives and we'll have a chat," he says. "There's only about nine of us and we do have some banter. I'm always up for a laugh as I've never treated life seriously. I like to muck about and have some fun. Then the jobs come up on the screen and off we go."

He was used to getting value for money when buying players and used the same skill in buying his most useful business investment – the on-board navigation system in his van. It helps him get around, specifically the nooks and crannies in London's centre. "I knew this job would involve going to London and these days I have to use glasses for reading," he says. "It's only six miles across central London but when you look at a map it can be mind-boggling. So I thought I'd get myself a satellite system. Then, if I'm going to somewhere like the Savoy Hotel, I press a button and it goes straight through to the control office in Bedford. They're mostly girls there and they're all lovely. They say 'hello Geoff, where you going today?' I give them a post-code and they send the route directly down to the vehicle. I don't use it all the time. But there are some streets I'm not familiar with, especially in the City. And sometimes, if I'm out in the middle of nowhere, I'll ring up and speak to Rebecca or Lisa and I'll say, 'just get me home'. So they do, straight to the door."

His boss when he started his current job was Marilyn Rogers and she would be at Post Haste to greet him every morning. "Geoff was a very cheerful, happy-go-lucky chap," she says. "He'd always be the one to brighten up a dull day and was always cracking jokes. He liked a laugh but was a good listener too. If you ever wanted to talk to him about anything he'd be there for a chat. He was excellent at his job too and would never turn one down. He'd go anywhere he was asked to go."

By the time he bumped into Bates, Chapple had established himself in his job, having been working for around six months. He had also got himself involved in football again, although not as a manager and not at a level one might expect of such a high-profile figure. While he had shied away from the glare of publicity and was determined to maintain his lifelong pledge of never having applied for a job in football, Farnham Town, a modest Combined Counties Premier Division outfit, had become the beneficiary of his knowledge and experience. "I was born and bred in Farnham and they've struggled ever since I've known them, which was when I made my debut, aged fifteen, as an inside forward," he says. "Anyway in early 2003, after I'd left Woking, I went down to watch them play a few times, just browsing. I was asked by a couple of people there whether I was doing anything and it transpired I was prepared to help. But not in the dressing room. I was willing to show them standards on the proviso that at any given time I may have said 'I'm going back into football', albeit in commercial matters or whatever. That was fine with them."

Keith Haskell, chairman of Farnham Town at the time, can take his share of the credit for getting Chapple to help out. "Geoff had finished with Conference football and he came to watch us on a couple of Saturdays," says Haskell. "I went over one day and said 'hello' and asked him whether he'd thought about getting involved. He said 'I might do' and in the end it happened, although to be honest it wasn't a difficult sell. He's a local lad who is a bit of a romantic and I think he was looking for something to do on a Saturday. I'm surprised nobody has come in for him but I'm not sure how much of that is his doing. He's tasted management, thoroughly enjoyed it but is happier now to take a back seat and have a quieter life."

Chapple has been literally putting something back into the grass roots of football, working to maintain Farnham's pitch. "It wasn't unusual for the two of us to be down the club at 8.15a.m. on a Saturday doing the ground," says Haskell. "Geoff's done an awful lot and it's not much fun sitting on a tractor in the freezing cold for four hours at a time, knowing that your team is going to lose 4-0 and it would be the same again the following week. Geoff's been more of a consultant and we've never pushed him to get involved with the team. Probably the club wouldn't have had the problems we've had on the pitch if he had taken over. But I always felt we owed it to him not to put him in a difficult position as he'd built up a good reputation over the years and I didn't want to put that at risk. We'll wait for the day when Geoff tells us he wants to do it." It might be a long wait.

One of Chapple's notable accomplishments was to find Farnham Town FC a sponsor. "I phoned a chap who I knew from Kingston and who lives in Basingstoke," he says. "He said to me 'for all the pleasure you have given me in my life I would be only too pleased to sponsor the club'. He paid it just like that, a few thousand quid all up front, something Farnham had never heard of or ever seen before. It allowed us to get some kit and tidy the place up. Now I'm really just helping out on the board. It's a small club with a lot of apathy. When I first came along,

Keith [Haskell] had high standards, which I liked. The club are still trying to do things on the pitch and even though I know a better way I don't tell them. I just observe and watch. They are never going to go anywhere and that's the way it is. You could go down Farnham High Street and ask twenty people whether they know where Farnham play football and probably only one would say 'yes'. I go back to my Woking days in 1984, when there were only eighty-seven people there, and I suppose the same answer would apply. Things have moved on since then."

This is where Chapple's love of his home town club glows like a beacon. While he admits he is probably too proud to manage at Combined Counties League level, he is not averse to his early Saturday morning routine of cutting the grass, marking the pitch and generally tidying up at Farnham's quaint Memorial Ground. "I went to school with a lot of them there," he said. "If ever I have a spare five minutes I go down to help. If something wants doing I believe in getting in there and doing it myself. Then people look up to you. That's how 'Geoff's red army' started at Woking. I spent all Sunday morning cleaning that ground after home games. In the end there were twenty people helping out. I gave them a biscuit and a cup of tea and they thought it was great to be sitting there chatting to the manager. I'm not too proud to do that. Now I believe Woking are paying about £400 to get it done."

Out in all weathers on Farnham's pitch at weekends, regular soakings are the norm for Chapple. There's plenty to keep him and one or two others occupied. On just one occasion he took over team duties, away at Frimley Green in the 2004/05 season. It wasn't a task he relished, with the side experiencing regular heavy defeats. "We drew 0-0 and got a point after the team had been losing every week," he beams. "That was marvellous. It was like winning the World Cup. It's not the best standard and Farnham escaped relegation that year because they ran about. That was one of my old coach Fred Callaghan's favourite sayings, 'run about'. I told the local press once that the football at Farnham was appalling. I thought it was off the record. I was given some stick for that by some people at the club but I told them at least the truth had been printed."

But the Nationwide Conference is never far from his mind. And he still thinks there is a place in the game for his style of management, even in the days when ex-pros such as Nigel Clough, Mark Wright and Glenn Cockerill are making their way in football's equivalent of Russian roulette. He also refuses to accept the criticism that he never gave youth a chance when he was managing Woking the first time. "I didn't, allegedly, have time for kids," he says. "But actually I did. It's just that I needed to move Woking on and quickly. Going back to the Isthmian League days, you always had to have a team that was good enough for the league above, to keep looking forward." Getting his hands dirty on the training field was never his style either and he is quick to admit: "I had no interest in coaching. Coaches are coaches and managers are managers. I always had a coach that knew how I wanted to play the game. But for me to do it? No way. I didn't want to run about in a tracksuit. That's hard work isn't it?"

Chapple has few regrets about his involvement in football but the nature of his current job means he has plenty of time to dwell on certain aspects of his career. Inevitably for a man who won the FA Trophy an incredible five times, Wembley Stadium is very much at the forefront of his thoughts and he admits to having flashbacks on his way around the UK. "Apart from the long hauls I'm always out and about in north London too," he says. "And I watched the new Wembley being built. To be honest I felt like driving in there each time I went past. I've often stopped to have a look around at the site. It's weird but I could have gone and sat in the old Wembley Stadium for hours when it was empty. That's what it meant to me." As a schoolboy of fourteen, Chapple wrote an essay about the two things he wanted most in life. One was to play at Wembley. "I never did play there but I managed the next best thing," he says. "And the other ambition, for some unknown reason, was to own a BMW. Well I've had about five of those. So I've achieved something."

While he still has the golden memories of the stadium, BMWs are merely possessions not worth a jot in the grand scheme of things. Far more meaningful, and a possession of sorts, has remained a constant for Chapple since February 1993. That is his thirteen-year-old daughter Lucy – a shining beacon in his life. She takes up much of the spare time he makes for himself. "She is the love of my life, my little princess," he says with pride. "Lucy is the one shining light that gives me the purpose to go on. I don't mean I want to end it or anything like that. But she keeps me going. And she likes things, so I spoil her rotten, like most dads. She likes coming to the football at Farnham. She's not silly either. When kick-off time comes around she says 'daddy, this is the time when you'd rather be in the supermarket'. She says that because of how bad the football is. She knows."

Chapple's relationship with his wife Sally, who he married in August 1991, went sour in 1997, just after he had left Woking FC the first time. He believes leaving Kingfield, Woking's home ground, was an event that had a bearing on her decision to leave the matrimonial home. "We still speak but that's about it," he says of Sally. "We divorced when Lucy was five. It was a bad moment in my life. I didn't see Lucy for six or seven weeks which, as any father will tell you, was hard. The first time I saw her again in all that time we were driving up the M3 and I was taking her to Thorpe Park. She was very quiet. She had a little blue hat on, with a rim. I asked her whether she was alright and she looked up and her hat was full of water from the tears. It broke my heart. And I remember that day, every ride she went on she was looking for me at every opportunity."

The day Lucy entered the world was a special one for Chapple. "It was a proud moment for me when Lucy was born," he says. "And we now have some quality time together. She throws her wobblys like all teenagers do but I love her to bits." Chapple was so devoted to his daughter that in the early days of his Kingstonian career, during the 1997/98 season, he'd allow her to go in the dressing room while he was giving his team talk. "The dressing rooms were big at Kingstonian and I'd push her out the back where she was out of the way a bit," he says. "She loved all that. It's funny how kids react. She's not so keen on Woking but it's probably because she thinks it's a bad word. But she loved Kingstonian and they made a fuss of her there."

Lucy recalls both clubs well, although she naturally has clearer memories of Kingstonian because it was more recent. "Dad used to allow me in the changing rooms but made me sit in the showers while he was talking to the players," she says. "The club was full of people who were always there to help and the atmosphere in the crowd was terrific. The people were very kind to me and it was a shame to say goodbye in the end. Dad was noticed wherever we went and people would say 'there's Geoff Chapple'." Contrary to her father's belief that she doesn't like Woking, Lucy says: "Woking FC was a wonderful place and the people and the players were the best ever. With dad going to Wembley three times it makes Woking special but winning three times there makes it even better. The music blaring out Tina Turner's *Simply the Best* is something I'll never forget but the best song was, 'Big Fat Geoff's barmy army' which was sung over and over again by the thousands in the crowd. The open top bus rides were a brilliant memory for me too but the best memory was running through the sprinklers with my friends on the Kingfield pitch. Woking is a brilliant place and I'll never forget it."

Chapple is famed for wanting to play football the right way; the ball played along the deck with intricate passing moves. Whether or not his teams were successful – and mostly they were – they performed a brand of football that had the punters coming back through the turnstiles wanting more. While he may have lost touch with Conference football, no longer going to watch games, he loves taking time out to see the very best perform at the highest level. "I'm a bit of a Blues [Chelsea] fan," he says. "Only because I used to go when Ossie [Peter Osgood] and the like were coming through. But I do find it a bit sad about the money situation at the club now. They can buy anybody they want. The money thing has turned it a bit sour for me. You can blame Sky TV for ruining football but I've got Sky and I watch it, so who am I to condemn them? I've done a bit for Sky too and could have done a bit more if I wanted but I chose not to. As much as I support Chelsea, the one team I do love to watch are Arsenal. They play beautiful one-touch football on a tight pitch. The way they do it is fantastic. They can't do it every week, but nine times out of ten they do. Thierry Henry is fantastic and is one player I wouldn't hesitate in paying to watch. But he's only fantastic when he wants to be. He has his days, just like Mr Buzaglo [Tim, former Woking hero] used to have his days. Sometimes Tim would say 'I'm too tired' or 'my wife hasn't fed me enough grapes'."

Chapple still eyes up Woking and Kingstonian's results and wants them to do well. And he isn't bitter towards the Cards, despite his sacking still fresh in the memory, and can now view them objectively. "The set up is still the same, in as much as the Kingfield ground is the same," he says of Woking FC. "There's more money involved now of course and they are very fortunate to be where they are with Chris Ingram as owner. They may have gone under like some other clubs without him. I knew the situation when I was there. And I know Chris will be taking his money out soon, but hopefully they'll be self-sufficient then, if everything else comes off. Until I was invited to go along and watch the FA Trophy match against Stafford Rangers [February 2006], I'd only seen Woking play once since I left and that was on the telly. Unfortunately they didn't turn up that day against Aldershot and lost 4-0. I really can't comment other than that. If I hear anything it's that they play a bit direct. It's not sad. It's only that I was first influenced by the old Tottenham push and run side, when Bill Nicholson was manager. As a fan I'd want to go along to Woking to see it played on the floor, but it isn't up to me now. The manager will decide that. If that person wants to play a direct route then I haven't got a problem with that. I don't criticise other managers too often."

There was an exception though. "The only one in my time I didn't like, although in fact I quite respected him really, was Stevenage manager Paul Fairclough," he says. "He would never let the word Woking be mentioned at Stevenage. I knew that because people in their camp were ringing me up and telling me about it. The rivalry built up from the mid 1990s between the clubs and it's still there now." For Fairclough those days when Chapple always seemed to get the better of him have stayed with him. "Geoff was a bloody ogre," he says with a wry smile. "He was always a thorn in my side but I admired him from afar. When I came on the scene he was 'the Daddy'. We had some tremendous games but Woking always seemed to win. The one that really hurt was the FA Trophy semi-final [1996/97]. They played most of the second leg at our ground with ten men but Darran Hay scored for them and he invariably did well against us. Woking were magnificent in holding on in that match and it went to a replay at Watford where they beat us, which was typical of them. That defeat broke our hearts."

Stevenage achieved something Woking have never done though. They won the Conference in 1995/96 and Fairclough had his moment to savour against the Cards during that season. "We had played Woking a few times by then but I remember the day when I felt the curse had been lifted," says the man who later went on to become the England semi-professional team boss. That match was on 8 April 1996, when his side thrashed Woking 4-0 at their Broadhall Way ground on the way to the Conference title – pipping Woking by eight points. "That was a defining moment for me," Fairclough adds. "I just decided to change my tactics on the day and it worked."

As for Chapple the man, Fairclough continues: "Geoff was a real character. Not a tracksuit man but a whisky and dry ginger man just before kick-off, so I'm told. He had a style that was quite unique and we had a mutual respect for each other." Both men later had a similar experience too. They both went back to their beloved clubs having left them, Chapple to Woking and Fairclough to Stevenage. Despite both of them trying to revive old glories, it didn't work and Fairclough reflects on Chapple's situation with real empathy. "Geoff has taken a few hits from a few people he thought he could trust and I know what he went through," he says. "I was seduced into going back to Stevenage and then the seducers turned. They say you should never go back and perhaps they're right. But people like Geoff and I like to prove other people wrong. I'm glad he's still well and who knows whether he'll manage again. I think in the right circumstances he could wave his mercurial wand but I don't know whether he has the hunger for it anymore."

Fairclough obviously looks back on those monumental clashes between the Cards and Stevenage as someone who was proud to be part of such epic battles and Chapple too thinks often of those times and the relationships he made. He still keeps in touch with former Woking star Scott Steele, giant ex-Kingstonian keeper Steve Farrelly, Buzaglo, David Leworthy and a few others. "You have to remember that in football you acquire plenty of acquaintances but not a lot of friends," Chapple maintains.

He has acquired adversaries too and one of them, former Enfield and Aldershot Town boss George Borg, cannot understand the powers that be at Woking Football Club for letting Chapple's talents go to waste. "I think it's disgusting," says Borg, who has never been short of an outspoken comment or two. "That club should have made Geoff a vice-president or given him an ambassador's role in some capacity because he made them what they are today," he adds. "The fact they haven't done that is a load of rubbish. He was a real character and I can't speak too highly of him. As most people will know, I don't give out compliments too easily but I make an exception for Geoff. I'm sad for non-League football and League football that he's no longer part of the game."

Having now turned sixty, Chapple lives on his own in a three-bed semi in Farnham and is satisfied with his lot – if not entirely happy. He hasn't changed much in appearance over the years although his heavy frame – which brought him that affectionate nickname 'Big Fat Geoff' – has filled a little as the years have worn on. Sitting in a van for hours hardly helps while, by his own admission, running has never been a hobby of his. His relaxation therapy still involves a cigarette in hand and his ruddy complexion and cheeky smile remain. So does his quick wit. And his senses are as sharp as a tack, even though his memory can play tricks on him occasionally. He can be forgiven that surely. After all, it's not easy differentiating between five Wembley finals for instance, when most mere mortals might just have the one to reflect upon.

As far as his personal life goes it might well have turned out differently for him. But he would be hard pushed to have expected a better deal when it came to his football management career. It was a vocation that started out from humble beginnings while growing up in a now prosperous Surrey town. But way back then, neither he nor his family could possibly have predicted where life was going to take him.

2

Windsor Safari

'A minor operation is one performed on somebody else' – Victoria Wood

"I think I'd prefer to be with you when you take the phone call," said the ward sister to the Windsor & Eton footballer who was lying prostrate in front of her with a broken leg and feeling as low as one could get. The muscular midfielder, who was decked out in his team's brand new kit, worn for the first time at Harefield United that Saturday afternoon, took it from the tone in her voice that it was to be anything but good news. His perception did not fail him. The person at the other end of the phone informed Geoff Chapple that his father, Bill, had died of heart failure a short time before, at around 3.40p.m.

It might have been just coincidence. It might have been fate. But at the moment – almost to the minute – that Chapple had suffered the worst injury in his football career, his beloved father had passed away. It was 8 March 1980. Suffering from the pain of his injury, Chapple admits his low ebb cushioned him from the heartbreaking news about his father. "Hearing of dad's death was a real life changer," he recalls. "But I felt so low at the time I don't think I could have felt any worse. I'd broken my leg and all I wanted to do was play football. My dad dying was very unexpected, although he'd been in hospital for two days. I'd been in to see him on the Friday and he was telling the nurses 'this is my son and his girlfriend Michelle', because I had two girlfriends at the time – Michelle and Jane. When the news came the next day I felt at rock bottom anyway, so in some ways it made it easier for me to accept."

But there was a moment of humour amid the physical hurt. Chapple's injury had come thanks to an accidental collision with Windsor team-mate Bobby King. It had been a wet pitch and both had slid for the ball from opposing directions before the sickening impact. "I was a bit slower than Geoff in those days," says King, a firm friend of Chapple's over the years. "I'd gone to tackle an opponent. Geoff was coming from the other way and I completely missed the player but took Geoff full on. He always prided himself on how strong he was in the tackle because he had muscular legs but I always joked that mine were stronger. That tackle proved it." The leg wasn't the only thing of Chapple's King broke that day. "As Geoff had gone to hospital, I drove his car back to Farnham for him," King explains. "I wanted to adjust the seat because I was taller than him. But I couldn't do it and in the end I forced it so hard the seat came off in my hands. When I started to drive it I was moving about all over the place. He loved his car [a green BMW] so I felt a bit bad." Chapple takes up the story. "Bobby came in to the hospital later and said 'sorry I broke your leg Chaps but I've broken your car as well'. He'd gone and busted my bloody car seat, I couldn't believe it."

While these days medical facilities in football are on hand to cover every eventuality, the 1980s were primitive when it came to anything other than a cold sponge. Following the incident at Harefield's Preston Park, Chapple recalls: "Brian Caterer [the manager] had come on to the pitch and was rubbing my leg even though I'd broken it. When I stood up it was like an electric shock going through me. In the ambulance the bloke said to me 'I don't think you've broken your leg guv', but the doctor came round at the hospital and confirmed the worst. They plastered me right up and I was in a ward with Tony Booth, Cherie Blair's father. They reckon he'd come home pissed one night, climbed in the back window, fell arse over head, knocked the oil stove over and set himself alight. He was bandaged from head to foot and we were learning to walk on crutches together. The sister was always telling me to get down to the hospital gym with old Tony. He was down there messing about on crutches but you couldn't see him. Just his bandages."

Chapple began what he thought were the first steps to recovery, but what followed was a real shock. In reality he was about to take a big step backwards. "The sister had said to me as soon as I could get up and down these particular steps I'd be alright to leave," he says. "But three weeks later, having been to my dad's funeral on crutches, I was back in hospital." He had been strapped so tight that a thick blood clot had formed on his lung. As a result blood began flowing freely out of his mouth. "I had my right leg in plaster and my right arm in a drip," he says. "I knew how bad it was when they put me in the ward because I was right next to the sister. As I got better I moved further and further down the room."

And although his broken leg eventually healed, one thing was certain, Chapple was finished as a footballer. Although he made a brief return at Farnham Town, merely for the love of the game, the sport in which he'd wanted to excel since he first kicked a ball in his back yard, had passed him by.

Those first recollections of his love for the game came in a part of Surrey that has shaped the life of Chapple the man, as well as Chapple the manager. Apart from a brief spell in Alton, the town of Farnham has been his home for all of his sixty years. "I've never wanted to leave," he volunteers. "I'm one of those old fashioned guys who never leaves anything. It's like football clubs. I'll stay there for life. I anticipated staying at Woking forever. I thought I'd be selling programmes there at the end of the day. But things happen and you move on."

Chapple was born in Farnham Hospital, Old Park Lane, on 7 November 1945, to "a poor family". Bill Chapple and Maisie, Chapple's mother, both appear in the official history book of the town, written by the then editor of the *Farnham Herald*, Peter Thompson. "Farnham remains firmly independent of spirit and has a rich panoply of architecture," wrote Thompson. "It's proud of its clubs and organisations and proud of its record in charity work. The town owes its growth to the development of agriculture in medieval times. Time and progress has not always been kind to Farnham but it doesn't wallow in the past or fret about the future. It does have problems in preserving the best of its heritage and accommodating the needs of the present. But what I see is an alert, vibrant town, which is always trying to present an attractive face to the world."

Just like Farnham, Chapple's mum and dad did not have time to wallow in the past or fret about the future. They were too busy making ends meet. What they did do is project the same attractive slant on life that their home town attempted to do, despite their humble surroundings. Bill worked at the local brickworks and had the relative luxury of having a house that went with the job. Maisie was a jack of all trades and a workaholic. Their home had no telephone, no central heating and was a mile and a half from the town centre. Between the two of them, their hard work and commitment in providing for young Geoff saw them keep their heads above water. "We were out in the sticks and I used to wake up to the sound of combine harvesters which was nice," says Chapple. "We had some rough winters back then and when it snowed you had to put polythene bags over your shoes if you were walking to Farnham to meet your girlfriend or something. Dad used to ride a bike because he didn't have a car. But having said that, I never went without and managed to go on all the school trips."

That school was St Andrew's in West Street, where he was often taken, kicking and screaming, by his mum. On occasion she had to take him home again, such were the problems she had in getting him to settle. There was never any doubt as to who was in charge of the Chapple household. "Mum wore the trousers," says Chapple. "Dad was very quiet and a good footballer. He was also well known for his dart playing in Farnham, although he wasn't a drinker."

Chapple's deep bonding with his mum grew from the day he was born. A day when both were very ill. "It was a life and death situation," he says. "Mum was in hospital for a long time afterwards. She went septic before the birth and the doctor said to her – and she always reminded me of this: 'Mrs Chapple, the best thing you can do is come back and have another child in a year's time.' She said 'no way' and went through with it, despite the dangers to both of us. When she said 'no' she meant it."

While the Chapples senior were keen on sport, they were also intent on ensuring their son had some company, even though the conception of another child was never an option given the complications Maisie endured in giving birth to Geoff. So they embarked upon the adoption route and at the age of five Chapple got a brother, Keith, who was two years older than him. "Keith had a bad start in life and was left in a shoebox in London," says Chapple. "As time went on he grew up, got married and joined the army, before moving to New Zealand. We lost touch until recently."

The two brothers were in the early stages of planning to meet. But it was destined never to happen. At the end of 2004 Chapple's first wife Linda, who he married in 1970 and with whom he had kept in touch, made a trip to New Zealand for a holiday, spending Christmas with Keith. "Before she went she had discovered some alarming news," Chapple says. "Keith had been involved in a car accident, had been hit and was in a wheelchair." Later came the shocking news of Keith's death. "I was in the throes of getting together with him again after all this time and was going to see him," he adds. "I was getting pictures together of Lucy. Then he was going into hospital for a routine operation in the February, got a blood clot in his neck and died. It was sad really. I hadn't seen him in such a long time and I was looking forward to seeing him again."

Incredibly, Keith Chapple had a Maori funeral, a rare occurrence for someone not of that origin. Chapple adds: "My next door neighbour is a Kiwi and he said to me, 'what was he, the Prime Minister or something?' He told me that for a white man to have a Maori funeral, Keith must have been somebody special." Investigations revealed that Chapple's long-lost brother had earned the equivalent of an MBE in the 'Land of the Long White Cloud', for services to the Maori people. Chapple felt pride at the revelation but Keith's passing was another chapter of his life closed.

Having had Keith to grow up with was a treasured gift for the young Geoff but his predominant memory as a child is of wanting to kick a football around at every opportunity. "We had a big bank at the end of our cottage," he recalls. "It was muddy. My dad and me would put a couple of sticks up and I'd be diving around. I got into football big time and mum always encouraged me. I got into running too and was a keen athlete. I even had my own athletics coach."

Chapple has fond memories of his parents and remembers vividly how his dad suffered with malaria for many years, having previously fought in Burma. His mother died in 1981, within fifteen months of his father's death, when she succumbed to the ravages of cancer. It brings back sorrowful feelings. "Mum hadn't been well and I was going away for a week with a mate," he remembers. "So I went to her doctor and told him I wasn't comfortable with going because mum had been poorly. He advised me to go so my mum wouldn't get suspicious and he assured me nothing was likely to happen to her until later in the year. We were in June at the time. So I went on holiday on the Saturday and blow me she was dead on the Monday. Some of the neighbours were saying things about me going away when I shouldn't have done. What they didn't know was I was desperate to get back. It was mum's birthday that week and the sad thing was I'd already sent the card from Spain and there it was on the mat when I got back. I was advised not to see her at the undertakers because they couldn't close one eye, which was horrible. But I went in and sat with her for half an hour anyway because I had to."

By this time, in 1981, Chapple was an employee of the Prudential Assurance Company based in Aldershot. He had started his working life as an apprentice printing compositor with a firm called Langham's, right in the centre of Farnham. He was aged seventeen and earned the princely sum of £2 a week. With a lot of his mates earning up to six times that amount, he left his three-year apprenticeship before it was halfway complete and joined the Post Office for a time, prior to becoming a Prudential representative, selling life policies, mortgages and various financial services.

The company was to become a big part of his life. Not only did it give him the financial security he needed, it allowed him to pursue his passion in life – football. Chapple talked a good game as a salesman and later, becoming a football manager enabled him to branch out with his network of clients. Combining the two was rewarding, although extremely tiring. His boss at the time was Alan Binfield, a man who knew he could rely on Chapple. "Geoff was one of my agents and he was a pleasure to work with," says Binfield. "He was good at his job too when he put his mind to it. He was always having to take time off for football because that was his main interest but in those days an agent worked from home and he seemed to combine the two no problem. In one year, 1989 I think, he was chosen to attend a star dinner in London and out of eighty agents he was top performer of the year." Binfield had seven agents to look after and adds: "Because I had seven it meant I would only see Geoff maybe one evening a week. But that was enough. Some of them needed a kick up the backside but not him. He didn't really need supervision. He had this charming manner and he could twist the ladies around his little finger. It wasn't like going to work when I met Geoff of an evening. With some of the agents I used to think 'I'm glad I've got that over with' but with Geoff it was more like pleasure."

Being Farnham born and bred, Binfield knew the Chapple family well and recalls his own time as an agent when the budding football manager he was later to work with was a lad aged just fifteen. "I used to call on Geoff's mother on a Saturday morning as she was a client of mine and it would be more of a social visit. We'd have a good chat and Geoff was just the same then. He was a good lad but he used to wind his mum up. She called him a few names but she was obviously very fond of him."

Chapple was happy at the Pru, despite the workload. "There was a lot of evening work and while football helped me get contacts, it also meant I was having to fit in my work on the same nights as training," he says. "I found myself getting home at eleven at night and I was still there at 7.30 the next morning doing my paperwork. I'd be drinking coffee after coffee just to try and keep myself awake. When the opportunity came to do the football full-time [1990] I let my heart rule my head. The Pru was a good life but it was demanding work. So I had a choice. Stick with my career or get involved full-time in football, which was my love." There was only ever going to be one conclusion and he took up Woking Football Club's offer to make football management his profession. He would earn £25,000 a year at Kingfield, the same annual salary he had received at the Pru. It was also the same amount of money he was on seven years later when he first left the Conference club.

Chapple had sampled his first taste of football management at Alton Town at the age of twenty-nine. "I was a senior player at Alton when I was asked whether I would take the job on after the manager left," he says. "I'd had no thoughts of doing it before then but I took it and combined playing and managing. The team did well and won the league and a couple of cups. Then we played Windsor & Eton in the 1979 Athenian League cup final." One of Windsor's joint managers was Colin Lippiatt – a man Chapple was to become synonymous with. "They were beating us 1-0," remembers Chapple, "and with about five minutes to go Brian [Caterer, joint manager and Lippiatt's brother-in-law] tootled off out of the stand. He changed from his tracksuit and got into his suit. He thought it was all over. But with a minute remaining somebody played the ball out to an Alton player on the right side of the park. It happened to be a bloke called Chapple, the player-manager. Anyway, I beat two blokes, cut inside, went around the goalkeeper and scored. At that stage the Windsor ribbons were on that cup. But you don't do that sort of thing because the game wasn't over. Brian comes out for the presentation and we're still playing because it's gone into extra time. He asked what was going on and was told we'd equalised. We then got a free-kick outside the box and I took it. It hit the wall, broke off right to a guy named Kevin Dennis and bang, he scored to make it 2-1. Alton had won the cup."

It was an introduction to Chapple that made an indelible impression on Lippiatt, who approached his future side-kick in the bar afterwards. "He asked me would I consider going to play for Windsor the following season," said Chapple. "But I was managing Alton, which is another club that's dear to my heart because I've got a lot of friends there. I told him we'd see what happened and then when Alton had no money to pay anyone at the start of the following season, four of us went to play at Windsor. There was myself, Chris Yates, who was one of the top non-League players around at the time, Ross McCulloch and the man who later broke my leg, Bobby King. What was a fairly decent side became a superb side. We went all the way to the semi-final of the FA Vase, the lot."

King recalls Chapple's attributes as a player. "Geoff was a strong and skilful midfield player with a good shot on him," he says. "People could never get the ball off him because he shielded it well and had a good first touch. He should have been a professional and the only thing he lacked was a bit of pace. I suppose the fact that Alton had beaten Windsor meant Brian and Colin wanted to sign their best players."

Life moved on at Windsor under Lippiatt and Caterer, and Chapple enjoyed his time as a player at Stag Meadow. He didn't miss the management side at that point in his life. There was to be plenty of time for that. Windsor were still an Athenian League side at the time and Chapple was thirty-four when Guisborough beat the Royalists in that FA Vase semi-final clash – just one match away from Wembley.

Then came Harefield and the end of his serious playing days at the age of thirty-five, when many in the game would be considering retirement anyway. Although, having recovered from his injury, a playing comeback of sorts, with Farnham Town, meant he had got himself back out on the pitch following his long rehabilitation. Farnham had been his first senior club and he had gone full circle. As he got himself involved again, club chairman Jimmy Butters urged him to sign a contract and become manager for the 1981/82 season, promising him £20 a week. Chapple agreed.

He called round to Butters' home to sign the paperwork, which was sitting in the lounge waiting for the deed to be done. "There it was sitting on the table, when the phone rang," says Chapple. "Jimmy goes through to answer it and he's chatting away while I'm reading the contract. Then he came back in and said 'that phone call might just interest you. It's Windsor & Eton and they've asked if they can speak to you regarding their manager's job'." Lippiatt and Caterer had left Windsor and gone to Woking. "Jimmy told me it was up to me to decide," says Chapple. "I told him I better talk to them. I hadn't known those two were leaving Windsor and I didn't know at that time they had taken most of the team with them to Woking."

Chapple went to meet Ken Cornwall, the Windsor chairman, and decided to take the job that would launch his managerial career. "It was uncanny that I should be in Jimmy Butters' home about to sign and then I'm on my way to Windsor & Eton," he says. "I could have signed that contract at Farnham. But then again Jimmy would have torn it up if I'd wanted because he was a good friend."

In joining Windsor Chapple had finally said farewell to his playing days. He'd had a good innings, realising his dream of turning out for Aldershot along the way, although he didn't make the progress he would have liked, playing only for the reserves and 'A' team.

When he arrived at Stag Meadow it transpired that a total of twelve players had departed for Kingfield, including goalkeeper Kevin Mitchell, John Mitchell, Jeff Chapman, Lance Cadogan, Kevin Hill, McCulloch and King. "I was in my twilight years and wanted to play for a bigger club," says King. "It was breaking up a bit at Windsor and we'd had a successful team so I went but I only lasted half a season there and ended up back at Farnham." One player Caterer and Lippiatt hadn't snaffled though was Yates, the jewel in the crown. "There I am at Windsor and I find myself with about two players, Trevor Baron and Yatesy, who was the star man and a mate of mine," says Chapple. "Colin and Brian took all those players with them but they didn't get him."

Chapple knew what was coming next. The newly appointed Windsor boss might have been wet behind the ears as far as management was concerned, but he wasn't stupid. Lippiatt knew he wasn't too but he tried his luck nonetheless. "The phone rings and it's Colin," says Chapple. "He was crafty. He said to me 'we still think you can do a job for us in the centre of our midfield at Woking.' I said, 'Col, I've had a broken leg mate.' Because although I had recovered, it wasn't enough that I could play at that level. But they didn't really want me. Straight away I knew what was going on. Their mentality was 'get Chapple, get Yates'."

Chapple saw through the scam. "I said 'thanks for calling Colin. Nice of you to think I can still do it. I'm not saying no but the chances are very unlikely.'" Lippiatt maintains it wasn't quite like that and adds: "I think Chris had already turned down an opportunity to go to Bournemouth at that time because he had a good job. It needed what I'd call a decent contract to attract him into a full-time environment. In all honesty if you thought somebody was going to be a draw-card because he was friendly with those sort of players, you've got that in the back of your mind of course you have. But it was no way premeditated to think that if we had Chapple Chris would follow. We just hoped that if we got Geoff first, others would be attracted to the situation."

Yates, who worked for BT, recalls it well. "I went around to Geoff's one day and he told me no way was I going to Woking," he says. "But I was happy to play for him anyway. Colin was still ringing me, asking whether it was the money and things like that. I just told him I'd been at Windsor a long time and I wanted to stay. I knew Colin was leaving the previous season. I'll never forget it. We were at Enfield preparing for a cup final and I was in the toilet. He came up next to me and said 'what are you doing next season?' I thought for him to do that an hour before a cup final was diabolical."

Yates stayed put, even though at the time he didn't know whether he was the only one to do so. As it turned out Baron was another to attend the first training night. "I think Trevor stayed for similar reasons to me," adds Yates, a natural goalscorer with a bit of pace. "I said to Geoff 'what are you going to do?' but he had lots of contacts and he began to pull some players in. He was such a good salesman he could persuade anybody to sign. There I was worried that the whole thing was about to disintegrate, but in fact the opposite happened. There was no doubt that Colin and Brian had put Windsor on the map to begin with because we had got to the FA Cup first round three times I think. But Geoff carried it on and they were great times, with some laughs along the way too."

Baron, who played under Chapple for ten years, recalls: "To be honest the reason I stayed at Windsor was because I wasn't asked to go to Woking. I probably would have stayed as I lived near Windsor's ground. And although I liked Colin I didn't get on that well with Brian. I'm glad I stayed because we had some good times under Geoff. Considering he didn't have a budget he did well with what were very ordinary players. In fact some of them were Sunday morning players." So Yates and Baron joined Chapple as he embarked on his first steps towards landing a job at Woking three years later.

It was another player who would one day link up with Chapple at Kingfield, Mark Davis, nicknamed Shaky, who was the saving grace for the new Windsor boss. "I got hold of Shaky and he helped me get that team together," he says. "He did wonders for me. He came with Frilly [Mark Franks] and we began to build a side."

Windsor had just won the 1980/81 Athenian League title and this was to be their first season in the Isthmian. In their respective opening matches Windsor were away to Rainham while Woking, with their ex-Windsor contingent, hosted Walthamstow Avenue. Both won 3-0 before Chapple's side "went through the divisions like a dose of salts." Chapple considered Cornwall and his colleagues "lovely people" at what was a homely club located on the edge of Windsor Great Park. He enjoyed his first sojourns in the FA Cup and met another man with whom he would later work in his career. Fred Callaghan, as manager of Brentford, masterminded a 7-0 thrashing of Chapple's men.

Whenever publicity reared its head at the football club Chapple was inevitably at the centre of it, with faithful coach Alfie Coulton at his side. The biggest moment in Chapple's career in Buckinghamshire came when Windsor – who had one or two of the Woking 'throw outs' return to the club – were paired with Harry Redknapp's Bournemouth in the FA Cup second round. "It was scheduled for a Saturday and the game was called off and put back to the Tuesday," he recalls. "The cup draw was on Saturday evening and I seemed to have developed a habit of coming out the hat first. "The voice said, 'Windsor & Eton or Bournemouth will play Manchester United.' Well it was a dream draw and I remember United manager Ron Atkinson saying that all he knew about Windsor was that there was a castle. We consequently played the game against Bournemouth, drew 0-0, then lost 2-0 in the replay. Then they go and beat United. I have spoken to Harry [Redknapp] since and he admits that he was worried before our game, having to play on Windsor's pitch, because it was such a leveller. Then Bournemouth tried to sign Yatesy who was a Farnham boy, but what they were offering him wasn't beneficial to him."

During that time Chapple stitched King up. "The papers were interested in what jobs we did outside of football," recalls King. "I was a money broker and Geoff told reporters I was on £60,000 a year. By the time the *Evening Standard* had got hold of it the sum had risen to £100,000 which was more than most First Division players were on. I got into trouble at work for that but I had my ten minutes of fame courtesy of Geoff."

Chapple was never one for drinking more than he could handle until one particular end of season dinner dance which the Duke of Edinburgh, the club's patron, had agreed to attend. "It was in a hotel right opposite the castle," says Chapple. "I was extremely excited that Prince Philip had agreed to come. It was one of those times when, although I didn't make a fool of myself, I was drinking as many shorts as I could. I was trying to free myself up as I was extremely nervous about meeting someone of that stature. He didn't stay for dinner but stayed for pre-drinks along with about three or four bodyguards who stood in the background minding their own business. He was like the man next door and we spoke for about half an hour, although I'm not sure what about because I'd had a few. I do remember he was talking about training because, like other clubs at that time, we were looking for a decent training facility. He was saying 'well, you could go up and train between the trees" and I remember looking at his working class hands and wondering what he was going on about because you couldn't train up there. Maybe it was the drink and I was imagining it."

The other memory that stands out from his heavily inebriated evening was sitting down to dinner when the waitresses were coming out to serve. "There was a lovely springy floor, super it was," he says. "All the waitresses had uniforms and wore heels. Then I remember looking up and seeing one of the girl's heels six feet in the air. She'd gone over and everything on the tray went with her."

They were good memories, albeit hazy ones, for a man who had maintained Windsor's upturn in fortunes. He had acquired a taste for cup runs, knew how to build a side and had enhanced his own personal profile in a short space of time. He wasn't to know it then, but his football career was about to take another exciting turn. It was a change in direction that would set him on the road to the pinnacle of non-League football.

3

One Man and His Dog

'I never climbed any ladder. I have achieved eminence by sheer gravitation'– George Bernard Shaw

There was never likely to be deafening applause at Kingfield on Saturday 29 September 1984. After all, however raucous their intentions, even if all eighty-seven supporters had stood close together to maximise the effect, that number of people in a football ground was hardly going to make themselves heard above the sound of silence. In any case in what had been a wretched start to the campaign, those Woking fans had nothing to cheer about and the arrival of a new manager, one they had probably never heard of, was not about to change their mood. Those supporters had seen their team lose their first seven games of the season, including an FA Cup defeat against Sussex League side Haywards Heath. The team had scored 5 goals and conceded 21 in that horror spell. There was no denying it, Woking Football Club and their suffering supporters were at rock bottom and, in the grand scheme of things, were about to sink even lower.

Geoff Chapple's arrival at the club, to take over from Bill Dodgin who had resigned, hardly raised a flicker of excitement among the Kingfield faithful and why should it? "To be honest I don't think any of the players knew who he was or had ever heard of Geoff," says Alan Morton, who was in the twilight of his career and whose eventual total of 178 goals made him Woking's second highest goalscorer of all time. "I think I was the only one as I had been around when he had played for the club a few years before." That less than 100 hardy souls had turned up for the new man's first match in charge was hardly surprising in the circumstances – there was never any reason to believe that the former Windsor boss would spark an instant revival. Added to that, visitors Clapton could

AN AGREEMENT made on the _1st_ day of _October_ 1984 between the Trustees acting on behalf of the Woking Football Club namely A E HILLS and P J LEDGER hereinafter called 'the Employer' and Geoffrey CHAPPLE a football manager hereinafter called 'the Manager' WHEREAS the Manager has agreed to serve the employer from the 29th day of December 1984 until the 12th day of May 1985 and thereafter until this Agreement shall be terminated subject to four weeks notice in writing from either side or by mutual consent

SIGNED by P J LEDGER and)
A E HILLS for and on)
behalf of the)
Woking Football Club)
in the presence of)

SIGNED by GEOFFREY)
CHAPPLE in the presence)
of)

Excerpt from Geoff's first Woking contract.

never be regarded as one of non-League's crowd pullers. The east London outfit had once enjoyed regular crowds of 4,000 at their quaintly named Old Spotted Dog Ground before the Second World War. In 1984 however, folklore has it that only the dog remained. The likelihood of finding a Clapton fan, even in Clapton, was rare; unless we were talking about the great Eric of course. It is feasible that Chapple's presence on that fateful day had somehow increased numbers at the gate. Clapped-out Cards against Clapton could quite conceivably have been a candidate for fewer than fifty supporters after all.

It is a time-honoured trait of the football fan that they want to be associated with a winning team, not an embarrassing one. For some Woking fans things had got so bad that it was time to visit the closet. Having emerged with the teams, Chapple surveyed the scene as he wandered to the other side of the pitch from the dressing rooms. The terrace, an iron rail with a wooden fence behind it (now known as the Chris Lane Terrace, despite the local entrepreneur having sold out to David Lloyd's empire), was sparsely populated to say the least. "It had been announced on radio the day before about me being manager but I'm not sure that many people would have taken any notice," says Chapple. "I remember walking across the pitch that day to a couple of ramshackle old flat benches. The club was in decline but even then I knew it had enormous potential. I remember looking at the bank behind the goal (now the Kingfield Road End) where a lady stood with her dog. She was an old school friend of mine and had come to watch. It was funny really because there were so few people there that she was the only person at that end. Every time the ball went over the bank I saw her dog disappear after it."

A Lee Frost goal separated the two sides and Woking had picked up their first three points of the season. But it was a false dawn, as they lost their next three games heavily against Leatherhead (5-1), Staines (4-1) and a Hitachi Cup defeat against Whyteleafe (5-1). "I remember Geoff played in that Whyteleafe game," recalls Morton, who was in midfield that day. "That was my one and only game because we were a bit short," says Chapple. "I didn't make the slightest bit of difference though."

Chapple knew he had to build, but his rescue mission was destined to fail – in that season at least. The previous season had seen the Cards play in Isthmian League Division One for the first time, having been relegated from the Premier Division at the end of the 1981/82 season.

And Chapple was their third manager since then as Dave Holloway, having taken over from Brian Caterer and Colin Lippiatt, then gave way to Dodgin. Chapple was about to find out that life wasn't going to be easy.

He had come to manage Woking after making a name for himself at Windsor. But the call from Cards' chairman Ted Hills had come as a surprise nonetheless. "I met Phil Ledger and Ted," recalls Chapple. "I went down for a chat and we ended up round the back of a tea bar. Eventually Ted said to me 'what do you want?' To be honest we were haggling over a fiver here and a tenner there. I was just listening really and we were talking minimal money like £50 or something. I'd always regarded Woking, even then, as a sleeping giant because I played there in the sixties. I knew it had potential, whether I was going there or not. I told Ted I'd need a couple of days to get my mind right."

Before he decided, Chapple wanted to see what he was letting himself in for. "At that first meeting Phil [Ledger] told me Woking were playing a local side, Godalming & Farncombe, on the Tuesday and he invited me over to have a look," says Chapple. "I told him I would come but I wanted to go in the ground unannounced so I could stand at the back of the old tin shed where the offices are now. I had driven in purposely about four minutes after kick off. But there's old Phil out there in the car park waiting for me. He said, 'hurry up we're 2-0 down already.' I couldn't believe it."

Chapple soon agreed to become manager of a team that had demonstrated a real Jekyll and Hyde character, able to perform brilliantly in one half before putting in an indifferent display in the other. A 3-1 lead at home to Bromley ended in a 5-3 defeat, while Boreham Wood were 2-0 up at half-time before going home pointless after Woking smashed in four second-half goals. The 6-1 home defeat by Walton & Hersham was as inept a performance as you could get. At least goalscorer supreme Morton was around to give his side half a chance, despite the team having frailties in defence.

Things did not look good with seven games of the season remaining. But out of nowhere four straight away wins looked to have done the trick for Woking who were now two points clear of Hornchurch – the Essex side being fourth from bottom and in the dreaded final relegation position. However, others around Chapple's side were winning too and it came down to the final Saturday of the season. "The three teams above us were all playing away and we were at home," says Chapple. "We're dead cert favourites to stay up because all we needed was a point. But they all won and we lost 3-1 at home to St Albans. We got relegated with 51 points and that's a good number of points to go down with. We had none when I went there. I don't really believe the saying 'it's a blessing in disguise' but at least we were where we should have been on merit. The table doesn't lie." Although he hadn't been there for the entire season, Chapple still felt the hurt of relegation and shared the despair of the club's second tumble down the football pyramid in three years. "It was terribly disappointing to go down and everybody was feeling it," he says. "It was a kick in the teeth. The fact it was in our hands made it worse. We didn't even have to win. A draw would have done. But we lost. And bang, we went down and it was a shock."

Chapple had made a lot of changes to the side and gradually got the players he wanted, even though it proved to be a team still not good enough to stay up. The disastrous start had put paid to that. Chapple had brought Windsor coach Phil Darren with him to Kingfield. A schoolteacher by trade, he was someone who shared Chapple's ideals. Together they began the rebuilding process. "Phil was a real gentleman and we worked well together," says Chapple. "But as things moved on he couldn't devote the time."

The Isthmian League Division Two South was uncharted waters for Woking but Chapple would prove to be the man to steer them back on to the right course. "We went up. Then, after a couple of years, we went up again," recalls Chapple. "It was getting big. We were getting players with a great will to win. We all worked hard and had the support of the committee. People were beginning to get interested. What was doing it was the football. The public liked to see the ball played along the ground. That's what I always wanted my teams to do, so we played the ball on the floor and the crowds began to pick up."

Club captain at the time, John Cassidy, is full of admiration for Chapple. "He never did me a bad turn," says the former central midfielder. "It was a real pleasure to play for him. Some players would always be on about how much money they wanted each season. Geoff would just say to me, 'I'll give you another tenner a week Cass' and that would be fine with me. You could see at that time he was building something. The quality of player he was bringing in meant he was going to give it a big push and he got the right players in at the right time. The older ones, including me, were eased out gently as the better quality ones came in."

Chapple remembers the early days at Kingfield with affection and recalls some of the tasks he was expected to do. "What I remember most was sitting at home with twenty brown envelopes, counting out fivers and doing all the money side of it myself," he says. "I normally ended up out of pocket. The budget was very low then, about £300 a week. As things got better it went up but in the early years it was real Dark Ages stuff." Having come from a financial background, Chapple was used to dealing with money but having a few handfuls of £10 notes to deal with was a far cry from the automatic system in place today. "If the budget was £500 they gave me £500 in cash," he confirms. "It was a good job I was trustworthy. It was terrible the way it was done really."

Most football managers have a relationship of sorts with their chairman and Hills grew on Chapple the more he got to work with him. "Ted became a good friend," he says. "But it was a real love-hate relationship. He never wanted to pay me but he'd always want to pay the players. Quite often we had rows in the club car park when I told him where he could stuff his job. I'd then get a phone call the next day and he'd say 'you'd better come and see me.' Then we'd make up. He was very supportive of me when he might have gone the other way. I might have been sacked because we got relegated, but he stuck by me even though I had some knockers at the time. I think every manager goes through a patch in their career at some stage when they get criticism. He was good to me though and a bit of a comedian with it."

Later on in Hills' stint in the chair, in the early 1990s, Chapple remembers a comical moment. "We went to one of the Conference grounds and had fish and chips on the way home," he says. "The directors all paid a fiver each so the players could have them after a game. Anyway, we'd finished them off and on the Sunday morning, we'd gone in for the working party I'd formed to clean the ground. Ted came in at half seven in the morning and he looked a bit strange. I asked him what was up. He was stuttering away telling me he'd finished his 'ffffish and cccchips' the previous night, put his teeth in the wrapper and thrown it away. He'd got no teeth left and had to fork out £137 for new dentures. He was a crafty bugger with money and there was another time when he owed me £400 so he paid me in coins from the tea bar. When I went in to the bank to change it all up it was £3 short. That was typical Ted."

Chapple knew when he took the job at Woking that his competitive nature would only allow for him to win, a trait he had continued from his life at the Prudential where he worked incredibly hard to be a cut above the rest. From there he went on to learn another valuable lesson – one that would stand him in good stead at the various functions he has been to over the years. "My district manager at the Pru, Doug Campbell, asked me whether I would be interested in going on a public speaking course," he recalls. "We went along to this thing and I think there were twenty people on it. We had to go in and introduce ourselves and there was a glass with twenty straws in it. We were told to take a straw out and the announcer said 'right gentleman would you just unravel your straw'. I took mine out and it had number one written on it. Well I knew what that meant. I was the first to go up." Chapple felt the tension, but he learned valuable lessons from it.

Unwittingly, it was another example of Chapple's luck when it came to being drawn out of a hat. When he was manager of Windsor, the Bucks side was the first ball out of the hat when the club drew a potential tie against Manchester United in the FA Cup third round. Then in 1991 the same thing happened when Woking drew Everton in the fourth round.

A turning point in Chapple's career as Woking manager came with the signing of a striker from local league side Weysiders. Tim Buzaglo, a quiet, down to earth man with dynamite in his boots, was the guiding light along the pathway to national star status – for Woking and for Chapple. There was no doubt his arrival at Kingfield in the summer of 1986 sparked a dramatic improvement in the Cards' fortunes. Brilliant Buzaglo scored 34 league goals out of the 110 Woking managed in his first season at the club, and he scored the all-important goal in the final match of the season against Whyteleafe, as Woking grabbed back their Isthmian Division One status at the second time of asking.

During the promotion campaign came an FA Cup fourth qualifying round tie at home to Weymouth, a match significant in that Chapple had persuaded a former England goalkeeper to turn out for Woking. Chelsea goalkeeping coach Peter Bonetti, sporting rather more grey hairs than in his playing heyday at Stamford Bridge, donned the Cards' no.1 jersey that day and Chapple remembers the circumstances with a smile. "Chris Lomas was out for a couple of games and so I managed to get Peter in," he says. "When I first saw him I said 'nice to meet you Peter, what do you need?' He answered, 'just give me the Christian names of the back four, that's all I want.' He didn't have a training session and he played great in the game which we won 1-0. Tom Spong, who was chairman then, said to me 'don't let him go, we've got to keep him and I'll pay his wages.' I said, 'alright Tom.'" Having blurted out he would fund the player's time at Kingfield, albeit only for a few games, Spong then asked the natural question. "He said to me, 'what's he want then, £30?' I said, 'Tom, you can add another nought to that'. Well, you can imagine his face. But he kept his money because we played Marlow at Kingfield one night and Peter was bloody hopeless. So that was the end of that."

The enormous input from Buzaglo that season – in what was his first at senior level – was not lost on his manager. "Tim came along through Mick Gowan, who was running the reserves," he says. "I remember meeting him in the clubhouse for the first time. He was a very quiet, unassuming lad but once he donned the red shirt we started to go to another level. He was outstanding. The things he could do were amazing. Give him the ball in any tight situation and he'd make something of it. You could mark him as tight as you liked but he'd still turn and beat you. As well as scoring goals he was a great provider as he'd get to the byeline and roll it back for the tap ins. He was brilliant and I only wish he'd joined a bit earlier."

Buzaglo wishes he joined earlier too. He'd only done so because Weysiders, from Guildford, didn't get promotion that year, meaning they didn't have a pitch to play on. "I rang Mick [Gowan] and said 'I've had enough of Weysiders, I'll come and play for Woking reserves,'" says Buzaglo. "Nobody had seen me play but in the end I didn't play one reserve game, I went straight into a first team friendly at Dulwich Hamlet. I don't recall Geoff ever giving a team talk. All he said to me was 'go and run around'. He continued to get players in and knew a good player when he saw one."

Buzaglo's laid-back attitude to the game, despite his exceptional talent, was legendary and Chapple recalls: "We played up at Kidderminster one day and before the game I was having a chat to Graham Allner, their manager. Suddenly Graham looked at me and said 'is he alright?' There was Tim asleep in the dug out. He was tired because he didn't like to travel. And he was never renowned for being a grafter. That's just the way he was. He never wanted to work hard in life or in football. Basically he was bone-idle."

Buzaglo doesn't refute the allegation. "I only ever got one rollicking off Geoff and that was when I fell asleep at Kiddie," he says. "He got me in the changing room in front of everybody and told me to pull my finger out and get out and play. But I did come across as lazy. I hated training Tuesdays and Thursdays and I hated travelling. That's why I liked Weysiders. If I wanted to go training, I went. If I didn't, I didn't. All I wanted to do was play football and I didn't think I needed to train."

Further evidence of the idle tag shines through in another story regarding former Woking coach Bill Stoves, who insisted the two forwards in the team, Buzaglo included, came back to defend corners by standing on the corner of the six-yard box. "I told Geoff I wasn't standing there as I was a forward and I was going to stand up front," recalls Buzaglo. "Later on Bill heard about it and said to me, 'if you've got anything to say about the team, you say it to me because I'm the coach.' So I said to Bill, 'Okay Bill, I'll tell you then. I'm not standing there.' I'd obviously got a bit braver by then." Buzaglo doesn't know to this day how Chapple came to be successful and adds: "He never used to say anything and left it all to his coach. For the first four years I just saw him as a manager who didn't say much, but he became more of a friend after that."

Life at Woking ended in disappointment for Buzaglo as a bad injury all but finished his career. That major blow for him – and Woking – came soon after his FA Cup heroics in early 1991. He suffered a cruciate knee ligament injury, courtesy of a tackle by St Albans' Bob Dowie, brother of former Northern Ireland international Iain. Buzaglo did play again, in the club's first Conference year in 1992/93. But he didn't last long, not least because he didn't like those trips the length and breadth of the country. He slowly drifted from the scene, having scored 151 goals in 244 appearances, including 20 as a substitute, but not before he had also carved his name in FA Cup folklore.

Chapple's old side Windsor & Eton provided the talking point in season 1987/88 – a year when Woking finished third, just outside the promotion places. For the average supporter, many games roll into one and end up being lost in a blur of obscurity. Sometimes it takes a moment of magic or a hatful of goals to ensure a particular encounter makes enough of an impression to remain lurking near the front of the memory bank. The FA Cup first qualifying round replay between Woking and Windsor on the 15 September 1987 was one such occasion.

Windsor led 3-0 with fifteen minutes remaining when the man who had been tormentor in chief, Mark Biggins, was inexplicably withdrawn from the action. Chapple made a switch himself, bringing on Richard

Buzaglo, brother of Tim, and Woking scored an incredible three times in the final eight minutes to take the clash into extra time. Three more strikes in the additional thirty minutes gave the home team a remarkable 6–3 win.

Biggins, a painter and decorator by trade and a real character, was only at Windsor for around eight weeks but he remembers that game well. "I'd been on holiday and had only played for a week before that match," he says. "So when we were 3–0 up with ten minutes to go I was feeling a bit tired and it seemed a good time to come off. Our manager thought I should have feigned injury and wasted time because as I was coming off they scored. So he blamed me but I just said, 'I suppose the other five were my fault as well.'" Chapple takes up the story. "When they took Biggo off they thought the game was won," he says. "The funny thing was a lot of people left early. The next morning the phone didn't stop ringing with people wanting to know whether the result was a misprint. They'd all gone home before the end and missed it."

Chapple knew that in Biggins he had seen a player that could give his team another dimension; a wizard on the ball in midfield who could bamboozle the opposition. "Biggo was a tremendous footballer and very clever on the ball," he says. "He was also one of your real characters, a real jack the lad. He always used to tell me I frightened him because I could go a bit wild. He always had an answer and was a non-stop chatterbox. He was a lovely lad and blended in well with the other players. He used to get kicked from pillar to post but he'd go round a bloke six times and make him giddy. I remember working hard to get him to Woking. We paid £2,000 for him I think and having him on board was great."

Anybody who saw Biggins play could not fail to be mesmerised by his plethora of tricks and knack of beating a man, not once but three or four times all in the same movement. "It was difficult at Woking for the first three months because I had my own way of playing," adds Biggins. "There were players leaving the club but not happy about it because they had enjoyed a comfortable time there. But gradually others came in and I began to settle down and enjoy myself. I think certain players thought that people like me shouldn't be allowed to do things wrong within the team structure, but Geoff just let me go and do my own thing. I liked that. When people paid money to watch you I always wanted them to walk away thinking they'd seen someone do something they couldn't do."

Chapple's wife Sally was a big fan of Biggins and the midfielder adds: "I don't think Geoff and I ever had a serious conversation. He used to say to me, 'some people thought you played well today but not everyone. Keep playing well because I might get lucky with Sally later, because you're her favourite player.' It was all silly stuff like that and the pair of us couldn't be serious with each other."

Ask Biggins about Chapple and it is clear he has genuine affection for the man. "He was very shrewd and knew a good player," he says. "He was never around at training though and in all the time I knew him I never saw him without a tie on. I never saw him kick a ball either. I used to joke with him and say the last time he kicked one must have been when they were brown with laces on. We didn't see him much on training nights and he'd have players queuing up outside his office for their wages afterwards but if he had been there he'd be gone by ten past nine. Fred [Callaghan, the coach] used to call him Lord Lucan. At training if Geoff came and had a look at what was going on Fred would say, 'do a bit lads, Lord Lucan's 'ere.'"

With or without Chapple on the training ground, Woking, with Biggins to the fore, finished third for the second successive season in 1988/89. But reaching the FA Cup first round was a significant achievement. Losing to Cambridge United 4-1 at home may not have been the best way to bow out, but there was no doubt it was the start of things to come for a side who would become famous within the competition.

Another promotion season followed for Chapple and Woking in 1989/90. Although they missed out on the Division One championship to Wivenhoe by two points, they conceded fewer goals, just 29 in 42 games, and scored the most, 102 to their rivals' 94. Yet again Chapple made the first round proper of the country's premier cup competition and once again they lost to Cambridge United, this time 3-1 at the Abbey Stadium, in front of 3,477 fans. "That was the time that John Beck was managing Cambridge and he had this thing about dunking his players in cold water," says Chapple. "They gave us cold showers that day which wasn't nice." Getting to the AC Delco (league) Cup semi-final was just another example of how far the team was progressing and the following year the club would hit the big time in the FA Cup – playing scintillating football into the bargain.

In the meantime, Chapple's world was becoming busier by the day as the pressure in both his football and business lives continued apace. In the summer of 1990, the club and the man himself knew that something had to give. "I was doing silly hours and the football club knew the hours I was putting in as manager," he says. "They knew how busy it was getting, what with sponsors' meetings and meeting people. Woking were becoming a big club and my work-load with the Prudential, together with the football, was becoming too much and they realised that. So we got together and the club said they thought it would be a good idea if I could be at Kingfield all the time. It was during a period when the club needed that profile, to have someone there full-time. I loved Woking, lock stock and barrel and I have no regrets in making the decision I did. I could have gone somewhere else in the mortgage game or somewhere different altogether. I'd have sold, wherever it was. The Prudential always used to say I could sell ice to the Eskimos."

The option of setting up home in Alaska and putting that theory to the test never materialised and so it was that Chapple went with his heart, not his head, and joined the professional managerial ranks in the game he adored. "In my first day in the job I sat in the medical room," he recalls. "I had no office, no furniture, nothing. I busied myself that first week in going out and seeing games, looking at new players and sorting out my sponsored car. Peter Braun and Rose Hurl were on the commercial side at the club and when the letter came through about the car, Peter thought it was for him. But I'd sorted it out myself. There wasn't enough work to keep me going at the start. But it was a new role and they hadn't had a full-time manager before so I had to make the position my own. Sooner or later there were secretaries coming in to help, with nice computers, and we were getting organised."

It was around that time that Chapple got to know Bill Sutton, who would become an instrumental board member, not to mention caretaker chairman, later in his time at Woking. Sutton was 'Mr Finance' at Kingfield, while he worked for Virgin Atlantic by day. "I think Bill was lonely," says Chapple. "I'd be watering the pitch and he used to come down of an evening and just stand there and have a chat. Sally [Chapple's wife] was there and Bill would be telling us about Virgin, this, that and the other. He knew he'd see me down there at night, that's how keen I was. It was through me meeting him in those days that he got involved with the club. Actually he was in it big time in the end."

Chapple was happy to take his salary at Kingfield, but the salesman mentality never left his side and he was keen to earn his keep. "One thing I always wanted to do was pay my own wages in terms of success and I think I did, in various things," he adds. Not even the most cynical Cards' fan could look back at Chapple's first spell at Woking and say he didn't achieve that aim, with the success he craved being just around the corner; during the very next season in fact.

4

A Fistful of Dollars

'Remember, we're all in this alone' – Lily Tomlin

The venue was the Moat House Hotel just off the M5 in Birmingham. It was close to midnight on Friday 4 January 1991. Woking chairman Ted Hills sat around a table with four of the club's senior players and manager Geoff Chapple. Money was the subject under discussion. There was a little more than fifteen hours to go before all six men would be involved, in one way or another, in the greatest day in the club's FA Cup history.

But a run in the world's most prestigious cup competition brings with it financial reward and having reached a third round clash against West Bromwich Albion, some Woking players wanted a bigger piece of the action. After all they had just knocked out three Vauxhall Conference clubs and felt, being an Isthmian League Premier Division outfit, they deserved any bonuses that were going begging. The haggling had been going on for some time. Chapple felt some empathy with his players. "Woking FC were getting bigger," he says. "There was more money around the further we went through the cup and the players weren't daft. They wanted a bonus, some sort of incentive if you like. To me money was never an incentive. It was just pitting my wits against whoever and wanting to win. I used to get so much pleasure out of that. But it was agreed that whatever the outcome the players would get appearance money and I hate that. We could have lost 10-0 and they would have still wanted money. The meeting developed and got quite serious as the evening went on. Eventually, at about midnight, there's myself and the chairman and three or four of the senior players."

Led by skipper Adie Cowler, the players wanted a certain amount, which was more than the chairman was prepared to give. Suddenly Hills decided enough was enough. "Right," he said. "Geoff, you're the manager. You sort it out. If you don't I want the reserve team up here by quarter to two tomorrow." Seconds later Hills was off to bed, the frustrated tone of his voice still ringing in Chapple's ears.

The matter had to be resolved. Somewhere lay a compromise and Chapple had to find it in the absence of his chairman. "Once Ted was in bed we sorted it because you have to have a bit of give and take," says Chapple. "It had probably been simmering for a while but at that time the club had a committee and it was difficult getting anything agreed. When a club is growing and bringing in more senior players like we were, money can be an issue. So the players got their money. But it wasn't thousands it was hundreds." By morning the manager was able to report to Hills that all was well and that a Woking first team would indeed be taking on West Brom later that day.

One player not involved in the negotiations was Mark Franks, who had been a key figure for Chapple at Windsor. He knew what was going on, but wanted no part of it. "To be honest I didn't care about the money and I think if push came to shove all the players would have played for nothing," he says. "I'm not sure how much support Adie had from the others but I had a feeling it was going to kick off that night. When all the players came down to dinner in the hotel we all had our jackets on and I think Adie was the only one wearing a tracksuit. That told its own story." That story was Cowler's act of defiance. By not conforming with the other players, he appeared to be spoiling for a fight, at least in Franks' eyes. "All I was thinking about was the game and at the time I was really nervous," Franks continued. "I used to throw up at half-time in games and was terrible in those days because of nerves. I remember Colin [Lippiatt] coming up to me and telling me he knew how I felt. Then he said, 'so I'm telling you you're definitely playing tomorrow.' I was so happy. It was great. Whether Geoff had told Colin to tell me I don't know, but I was able to sleep well because I knew I was in."

Prior to those goings on at the Moat House, and that momentous day at West Brom, Woking's historic 1990/91 cup run had begun with a 2-1 win against Bath City at Kingfield and was followed by three encounters with Conference giants Kidderminster Harriers in the first round proper. In those days, it was always the first round 'proper' or the fourth round 'proper' for the likes of Woking. Such was the Cards' standing in the eyes of the Football Association at that time they had even been chosen as one of a handful of non-League clubs in the competition to be exempt until the fourth qualifying round.

The three matches against Harriers attracted 9,091 fans in all and Chapple recalls the last of those vividly. "After the second game at Kiddie we tossed a coin to decide the venue and it seemed that Woking might not be going too much further because the luck favoured them and they won the toss," he says. He needn't have worried. A late Andy Russell header gave Chapple's men a 2-1 victory back at Aggborough on a night charged with emotion.

Chapple had forged a real friendship with Harriers' boss Graham Allner; a "really nice fella." For Allner, those three matches were when he believes "Woking really came to prominence" and he remembers his team – who went to the FA Trophy final that season – getting more than they bargained for. "I didn't know Geoff then but remember him being pointed out to me on the terraces at one of our matches in the run up to the FA Cup games between us," said Allner. "I remember him looking spruced up and like a professional football manager should do. Obviously he had built a brilliant side at that time. Seeing what they went on to do against West Brom, having beaten us, I remember feeling quite envious. Geoff used to have the same philosophy as me. If I didn't enjoy watching my team play then why should I expect anyone else to? I got to know Geoff well after that. He was a lovely man who I struck up a good relationship with. But he was single minded and when you were up against one of his teams you knew you were in for a real game."

The second round brought a third consecutive Conference side to Kingfield; Merthyr Tydfil from the Welsh valleys. Two of the visiting players were sent off as Woking, inspired by a brilliant hat-trick from Mark Biggins, crushed their opponents 5-1.

The draw for the third round saw the Cards being pulled out of the hat along with West Brom, who plied their trade in the second tier of English football. "There was a buzz happening at that time," says Chapple. "I didn't know what but I had the feeling something was happening. Gates were improving and things were moving. When the draw was made there was never any thought that the game was winnable. But I remember driving along the Hogs Back on my way home to Farnham and wondering what I was worried about."

Woking met Marlow in the AC Delco Cup on Tuesday 18 December and, possibly with their minds on the FA Cup, put in what Chapple describes as their worst away performance of the season. It was there he met the man he was about to go head-to-head with, West Brom boss Brian Talbot. "I spoke to Brian before the start of that Marlow game and his actual words to me, with which I totally agreed, were 'if my lads don't beat your lads, they want their arses kicking. After all they are full time professionals.' I thought it was a perfectly reasonable quote that nobody could disagree with. Anyway Brian had seen enough and left ten minutes before the end, but no sooner had he walked out of the ground we scored twice and won 3-1. He'd have driven back to the Midlands rubbing his hands with glee I would have thought."

And so to the day prior to the West Brom clash and with his fierce dislike of coaches – the four-wheeled kind that is – Chapple drove up to the Moat House in his own car with Sally and two long-time friends, George Priest and Sue Knight. Staying in the same hotel were Cambridge United, a team that had knocked the Cards out of the FA Cup twice in the previous three years. They had a third round date at Wolverhampton Wanderers. For his own third round appointment Chapple was completely at ease. "With the team we had I knew we'd have a go," he says. "But hand on heart I didn't think we'd beat them. They were in the old Second Division and we were in the Isthmian League. There was a huge gap of four divisions."

But West Bromwich Albion were not at their peak. They were no longer the First Division side containing the likes of Bryan Robson, Cyrille Regis, Brendan Batson and the late Laurie Cunningham. But for an Isthmian League outfit, they were formidable opposition nonetheless. Chapple checked out The Hawthorns ground on that Friday afternoon and was impressed with the stadium. "There was enough there to almost frighten you," says Chapple. "In fact the atmosphere alone was enough to do that."

The following morning, the day of reckoning, he made the short journey again, only this time there was torrential rain. So much so he had his doubts that the game, scheduled for a traditional 3p.m. kick-off, would be played. Everything was fine by the afternoon though and as he made his way up the tunnel around eighty minutes before kick-off, Chapple noticed something. "I walked past their dressing room," he says. "I looked in and saw three or four of their lads sitting around reading newspapers, not the match-day programme. I think I said to my lads that, in my mind, I felt the West Brom players thought we were just a minnow side from down south who had arrived for a pasting. Their players were totally relaxed, probably too relaxed. What with their mentality and our travelling fans, it lifted us. To have 5,000 supporters there backing us was something else, albeit they were tucked in the corner."

Chapple knew this was Woking's one chance at the big time and most Cards' supporters went to The Hawthorns believing it just to be a day out to enjoy, no more than that. "All I wanted was to give a good account of ourselves and hear nice things said about Woking," he says. The game started and Woking, even though as a team they were markedly smaller in physique than their hosts, grew in confidence as the match wore on. "We were 1-0 down at half-time but I was bloody pleased," says Chapple. "I can't remember what I said at half-time but it would have been along the lines of 'well done, we're still in it.'"

Hero of the day Tim Buzaglo struck a wonderful goal to equalise as Woking began to play a passing game that had the home team not knowing which way to turn. Graham Roberts and Gary Strodder, Albion's centre-halves, were finding Buzaglo a handful and, not long after, he headed a second. Woking were in front. "When the second one went in I remember thinking of all the permutations," Chapple says. "Then Tim scored his third and I kept thinking we could hang on for a draw here. It was crazy thinking like that at 3-1 up but it was because of the stage we were on. Then I was thinking what will happen if we win? What will happen to me? What will happen to the club?"

With West Brom fans turning on their own players and applauding the Cards, substitute Terry Worsfold added a fourth as Woking went into fantasy land. "Before I went on Chaps just told me to get on there and get a goal," says Worsfold. "So I did, although it wasn't enough for me to play in the next round." Chapple adds: "When Terry scored I remember him running over to our supporters and then my mind was racing as I knew we were going to be major news nationally."

The Baggies scored a late consolation but Chapple was right in his summation. His side's 4-2 victory was splashed all over the national papers. After running over to Buzaglo, Chapple was walking off with the hat-trick hero when he mentioned to his star striker that they should go up the other end and clap the home supporters who had come on to the pitch. "Tim agreed and some stewards came with us," says Chapple. "All of a sudden the West Brom fans picked him up. All I could hear was them singing 'sign him on, sign him on, sign him on.' That was special, they were so kind."

For Buzaglo, who was reluctantly whisked off to the *Match of the Day* studios afterwards, it was a special time too. "That was the best moment of my life and Geoff was with me all the way, probably because he was looking after me," he says. "We had a good relationship and he was good to me. As far as the football was concerned we played some fantastic stuff that day and we were so good at that time I wasn't fussed about playing anybody. But the attention I got for the two weeks leading up to the next round were the worst two weeks of my life. I hated every minute of it. But anything Geoff told me to do in that time I did, even though I didn't want to. One of my regrets is going public in saying Graham Roberts was slow. I didn't think I'd be playing against him again. But I did, for Marlow against Enfield. He'd remembered every word I'd said about him and gave me a right kicking."

Buzaglo also regrets missing out on the fun with his teammates after the West Brom win but while he never made it back to the dressing room, Chapple eventually did. "I'd only got two steps in when the players picked me up and threw me in the deep bath," says the boss. "It could have been dangerous. My heels slid along the bottom of the bath and I was completely under water on my back. When I surfaced I noticed that somebody else, with a jumper and slacks, had decided to jump in. That was Colin [Lippiatt]. I came outside the dressing room and there was a fella standing there. It was Chris Dyke [a local journalist who covered Woking FC for the *Surrey Advertiser*]."

Dyke takes up the story. "A large posse of excited reporters had squeezed into the press room but knowing Geoff as I do and having arrived with the Woking party, I managed to get to the dressing room area," he says. "I was greeted by a beaming but drenched Woking manager and I told him he was wanted upstairs for interviews. He told me in no uncertain terms he couldn't go up looking like he did. So under instruction from West Brom's version of Pauline Fowler, who had taken pity on him, he squelched towards the Baggies' laundry room. On the way he emptied his dripping pockets and handed me his keys, fags (or what was left of them), lighter, wallet, wrist-watch and a few quid in loose change for safe keeping." Chapple adds: "She was a nice lady in the laundry room and I was so elated I just stood there in the nude as she found me some kit to put on." After a while he emerged to undertake his press obligations and Dyke recalls: "He followed me upstairs to the waiting press corps. It was all rather surreal but it did give me a little exclusive. I don't think the sartorially elegant Chapple ever conducted a post-match interview in a pair of shorts again."

Chapple upset some West Brom fans in the process of giving his account of the day's events. "I came across as disrespectful because I actually said I hope we get someone decent in the next round," he says. "That was perceived by some people to mean West Brom were hopeless and I didn't mean that. What I should have said was, 'I hope we get a team from the First Division.' West Brom were fantastic on the day and I felt sorry for Brian [Talbot] who was sacked a couple of days later. I had a feeling he knew what was coming and it must have been horrible for him to go home to his family."

Buzaglo and coach Fred Callaghan had been whisked off the *Match of the Day* studios in Shepherd's Bush and Chapple was not too concerned that it was not him, as it would have ruined his night. "Normally one would expect to see the manager on the telly but I had friends with me anyway," he says. "The four of us, George, Sue, Sally and myself went for a meal after going back to the hotel and finding out Cambridge had won their match too. We found a nice little restaurant and when we got there about 6.45p.m. it was empty. But as the minutes passed it got busier and all I could hear coming from different tables was 'how did we manage to lose to that lot?' I was getting uncomfortable and so we hurried our meal, paid up and moved out as quickly as possible."

Dyke has covered Woking matches for more than a quarter of a century and for him there has never been a more special occasion than the West Brom match. "It remains, and probably always will do, my most cherished memory," he says. "It was the first and, I believe, the greatest, of all their FA Cup adventures. The Chapple-led apparent mish-mash of interior designers, van drivers, decorators, door fitters and bank clerks had been moulded into a formidable non-League force but were given little chance, even by many within Kingfield. Winning the FA Trophy in 1994 and seeing the team run out at Everton in the next round of the FA Cup were golden times, when watching Woking brought a lump to the throat. But never did those emotions escalate to so close to tears than in the aftermath of that Buzaglo-inspired victory at West Brom. My colleague from the *Surrey Herald*, John Whitbread, sat alongside me in The Hawthorns' press box and at the end he turned to speak to me and sensed I was having an emotional moment. He just said 'sorry mate, I'll give you a minute.' It wasn't just that Woking had beaten them. They played them off the park in an extraordinary second half. And it was made more special by the West Brom fans recognising it as a remarkable and historic achievement by a part-time team."

Flying Cards' winger 'Frilly' Franks, who played no small part in the historic victory, adds: "That team was superb to play in. And the style was so different to what we did under Geoff at Windsor when Alfie Coulton was coach. Alfie was allowed to do it his way and we played percentage football.

"I used to drop deep and clip balls into channels and we were very good at it. But at Woking it was just five-a-sides in training and all we did in games was attack. With five at the back I didn't have to defend and it took a bit of getting used to. I think Geoff got success through keeping players on edge. You never knew what was going though his mind. You could play eight games in a row and then he'd drop you. He did that to me at Cambridge United in the FA Cup the season before. There was a flu bug and I think I was the only one who didn't catch it, yet I wasn't even named as sub. I was almost in tears after that. But he got me started in non-League football and if it hadn't been for Geoff it may not have happened for me."

After that amazing win at The Hawthorns, the fourth round draw – the fourth round proper no less – followed twenty-four hours later. All connected with Woking Football club were packed like sardines in the clubhouse, waiting for the sixteen remaining ties to be drawn. Woking, who were not even in the Conference at that time, were in the mix. Incredibly the Cards were first out of the hat. The announcement almost blew the roof off the building. "Woking... will play... Everton!" Chapple and his team jumped for joy on hearing those words and their reaction was spread all over the national papers the following day. "At the time the draw was made there was so many bodies embracing each other and hanging off the ceiling it was incredible," he says. "What's running through your mind then is 'bloody hell, we'll get beaten 10-0.' Then there were thoughts of where it would be played and I knew that if it wasn't going to be at Kingfield then I didn't want it anywhere else other than Goodison Park."

From that moment Woking really had hit the jackpot and they were big news. "The build up was fantastic," says Chapple. "Everybody was in the public eye. I don't enjoy all that but you had to do it. Biggo [Biggins] was on the telly, Adie [Cowler] was on and Tim [Buzaglo] was filmed

The reaction as Woking were paired with Everton (from *Today* newspaper).

at work. The press never left us alone and the profile the club got was fantastic."

Chapple watched Everton twice before the momentous encounter at Goodison, the venue having been switched, and his boots were filled with fear on each occasion. Howard Kendall's team was packed with internationals including Graeme Sharp, Kevin Sheedy, Neville Southall and Kevin Ratcliffe. Chapple was getting nervous.

There was a noticeable increase in numbers in the Woking party for the Everton match, which was played in front of a crowd of 34,724 on Sunday 17 January 1991. Only Manchester United attracted more through the turnstiles at Goodison Park that season – and that included the derby clash with neighbours Liverpool.

Having received a warm ovation at Anfield on the Saturday afternoon, merely for being announced as in attendance, the Woking players stayed in Southport that evening in readiness for their date with destiny. This time bonuses had already been agreed at £750 a man for the majority of the squad and management team.

It wasn't money which concerned one particular player ahead of what would become the biggest match of their lives. "We'd decided on our squad and this player came up to me that night and asked me whether he was in it," says Chapple. "I told him it was bed time, but he told me he needed me to put him out of his misery one way or the other otherwise he couldn't go to bed because he'd never get to sleep. When I said 'yes you're in the squad,' he was so elated. It was Paul Mulvaney and, being a scouser born and bred, I'd made him very happy."

Mulvaney had not been so happy to have been left out of the West Brom squad though and this time it was Worsfold who was the unlucky one. "I was injured anyway," says Worsfold. "I'd got injured against Basingstoke the week before and I remember we were training up on Southport beach and I had a fitness test. I was struggling to shake it off but Fred [Callaghan] just said, 'I wouldn't worry about it Worsy, you're dropped anyway.'"

The day of the game arrived and there was to be another first. "It was something I'd seen but never been part of," says Chapple. "We were escorted by police motor cycles to the ground, through red lights and everything. I thought to myself, 'hold on, we're Woking Football Club. Is this really happening?' There were masses of people outside the ground when we got there and a lot were Woking supporters. I got interviewed up there by a radio station from back home and they said, 'if only you could see what is leaving this town today.' Apparently there were 125 coaches and as soon as I heard that I thought I'd love to have been in a helicopter above them looking down on it."

Everton chairman Sir Philip Carter proved the perfect host, wishing Woking all the best while taking champagne to the visitors' dressing room before the match. Cheekily he requested the Woking players consume some before kick off. "I'd liken that period of time to Christmas morning," says Chapple. "West Brom was always going to be special because it was the first, but this was massive. The players were all trying to grab programmes as souvenirs and I kept nipping down the tunnel to see how full the ground was. The players were saying 'can we go out yet?'

I'd be saying 'no, hang on we won't go just yet.' I was using up so much nervous energy running back and forwards to see how full the ground was. Eventually, at ten past two, I looked out and it was nearly full so I said, 'come on boys you can go out now.' They were all still in their blazers and slacks and I only did it so we could get the maximum effect in front of all those people who'd come to share it with us. It was pathetic really. But we hit that turf and it was almost as if you were walking with your feet six feet above the ground. The noise was incredible. Then it was a bit of a rush job to get back in and changed but we managed it."

The Sun newspaper had done a deal with Woking and reporter John Sadler had the privilege of sitting in the dugout along with the substitutes – all except Andy Russell who had to stand as there was no room – and Chapple, Lippiatt, Callaghan and physio Barry Kimber. "John wrote a nice piece," says Chapple. "We got a few hundred pounds off them. He said it was one of the best days of his life because it was fun."

Just like any other top club's pitch, the Goodison Park surface had a camber and Chapple remembers Franks scurrying along the left flank on the far side of the pitch and only being able to see his body above the waist. Forty-five minutes was almost up and suddenly Franks began to loom larger as he scampered across the pitch towards the dug-out. "He's come all the way over and said 'how long until half-time?'" says Chapple. "I couldn't believe it and told him in no uncertain terms there was a bloody great clock on the stand behind him and all he had to do was look at that. John Sadler was falling off his seat laughing." Franks recalls: "I didn't see the clock and felt a bit silly when it was pointed out to me. I think it was mentioned in *The Sun* the next day because Sadler thought it was so funny."

Cards' stalwart Lloyd Wye had seen that clock and remembers it for different reasons. "I remember the game was so much quicker than we imagined and after a while I was absolutely knackered," says the left back. "I had my hands on my knees and glanced up at the clock and noticed it said 3.18. I was thinking I can't believe I'm feeling like this after just three minutes. Then I realised it was the time, eighteen minutes past three."

Amazing though it seems now, the minnows of Woking were doing non-League football proud by holding the might of Everton 0-0 at half-time. It was a result that would have shaken a few people. In the end a typical Sheedy goal, swept in with his left foot, gave Everton the 1-0 win, although it was Woking who took the glory. "People were coming up afterwards and asking me for my autograph," said skipper Cowler after the final whistle. "Who the hell am I?" he added.

Despite his team earning a fifth round tie, Everton boss Howard Kendall was far from amused by his team's performance. *Surrey Herald* sports editor Whitbread, a close ally of Dyke's, recalls: "Chris and I managed to blag our way down to the dressing room area afterwards and Kendall was having a right go at his players. He was yelling how they'd been lucky to win it and how they'd almost embarrassed themselves. He was going absolutely mad and you'd have thought they'd have lost the game from the way he was acting."

Many believed that losing 1-0 was the best result the Cards could have got unless they were going to win, as a draw may well have meant a thrashing the second time around. Buzaglo agrees. "In those days you had one chance and one chance only," he says. "I'm glad we lost just 1-0 because beforehand people thought it was a 7-0 job." Chapple is not of that opinion. "Tim [Buzaglo] and Shane [Wye] came close to scoring and the best result we could have had was 1-1," he says. "We had fighters in the team and although it might have been more a second time, I would have liked a second chance. I was deeply disappointed to lose just 1-0. Everton were gracious in victory and gave us an ovation. But Howard [Kendall] said later if we'd have beaten them they certainly wouldn't have clapped us off the pitch. The Everton game kicked us off as a club financially. West Brom got us going but when we got that £90,000 from Everton, that's when the ground started to improve. That was the cheque that did it."

Inevitably Woking fell away badly in the league after their tremendous heroics in the country's premier cup competition. They had come off a huge high and landed in a trough from which they found it difficult to emerge. Chapple praised Callaghan and Lippiatt for doing their bit, but the strain of the cup run had already manifested itself in between the West Brom and Everton clashes. "We lost to bloody Basingstoke in the League and Fred [Callaghan] and myself had a massive argument which carried on down the tunnel and then outside the boardroom," says Chapple. "It was petty really and was all about what happened in the build up to Everton. Fred was a taxi driver and he took his taxi over to the snooker centre [next to Kingfield] and did something for the *Daily Mirror*. He was doing this and that off his own back and we had a bust up in the dressing room. No wonder we lost 2-0. We very nearly came to blows. The funny thing was Ted [Hills] was like a Punch and Judy puppet. He kept putting his head around the door saying 'now stop it, stop it'. Then he'd go out again and come back in and say it again. It was comical looking back."

There was no laughing in the next League match at home to St Albans on 2 February 1991, when Buzaglo went down under the tackle from Bob Dowie, which resulted in him missing the rest of the season and much of the next with cruciate knee ligament damage. It was no coincidence that Woking's season fell flat after that. "It was a crucial blow for Tim and for us," Chapple admits. "Much had been achieved as a club and there was plenty more expected. The gate receipts alone from the cup run meant we'd made some money and some friends as well. For Colin [Lippiatt] and myself it was good too."

Reflecting on the season, committee member Phil Ledger, a club stalwart of more years than he would care to remember, and who later became chairman at Kingfield, says: "The memory of West Brom will never be forgotten by us nor by their directors. I remember a few years later I was having dinner with Geoff at an England semi-professional game at Rushden & Diamonds FC. Brian Talbot was the manager there and he came up to our table and Geoff said something about the time when Woking had beaten Talbot's team at The Hawthorns. I'll never forget what Talbot's reply was as they shook hands. He said to Geoff: 'I do remember you got me sacked and I've never had the chance to thank you.' Geoff was puzzled and then Talbot added: 'I got £100,000 out of that and I put it in the bank. Now it's worth £200,000 so thanks very much.'"

Ledger and all at Woking were aware that the foundations had been laid during that historic 1990/91 season and the club were well and truly on the map. While they never achieved top level non-League status that season, they were about to embark on a record-breaking term that would get them there a year later. They even managed it without the injured Buzaglo; although what they had achieved in that unforgettable few months had been largely down to him and his colleagues, many of whom were unsung heroes. Chapple – not to mention history – would never forget the striker's indelible contribution, nor the accomplishments of his teammates.

5

Pretty in Pink

'If we don't succeed we run the risk of failure' – Dan Quayle

"We had a lot in common; she liked Chelsea and I liked Chelsea," he says, with the emphasis slanted towards the second part of the sentence. Well, one would expect a football manager to look for a kindred spirit when assessing the suitability of a new bride, especially when he never imagined he'd be taking the plunge into matrimony a second time. Geoff Chapple's first marriage in 1970, to childhood sweetheart Linda, had lasted five years. Taking on the mantle of husband again at the age of forty-five, this time to Sally, might have been wholly unexpected in the aftermath of his first break-up, but for him it felt right nonetheless.

That particular year, 1991, was a life-changer for Chapple in every sense. He had driven along that road to FA Cup glory at West Brom and Everton, and had basked in the acclaim only afforded to those who have accomplished great deeds. Now it would become a year when decisions would be the name of the game. Those decisions crossed the boundaries of his personal life, career and his passion. All three aspects of his world were intertwining and bringing with them a deep happiness and satisfaction that he feared had passed him by.

Leaving the Prudential for a full-time position in football management at Woking in the summer had been a big step, but one he was destined never to regret. In the latter months of the year, and then into 1992, he would also make some major decisions about his Woking players' limitations as he fretted over whether they might adjust to a higher level of the game.

In a similar way to his approach to switching professions, deciding to marry again had been an easy judgement to make, although it had by no means been a headlong rush into the relationship; quite the reverse in fact. Having broken up with Linda in 1975, Chapple was not expecting to find compatibility with someone else in the long term, and he certainly didn't envisage enlisting wife number two. Then he met Sally in his local pub, The Cherry Tree, in Rowledge, near Farnham. He had started to go there when a new landlady and landlord, Yvonne and Ray Cleminson, took over. Ray was someone he used to play football with – in trials at Portsmouth and at other times. "Having met Sally, we eventually became friends," says Chapple. "I used to give her a lift home and it was purely platonic. I didn't even get a peck on the cheek in those days, but the relationship grew and we got on ever so well and had a lot in common. She liked football which was great and we both liked Chelsea and it just seemed right."

They decided to get married but, in true stereotypical bloke's mentality, Chapple is not able to remember the finer details. "I couldn't tell you the date but it was on the Saturday before the start of the 1991/92 season," he says without a hint of self-reproach. "I remember it was a Saturday at three o'clock," he adds as if that will in some way justify forgetting his own wedding day. Granted, it was the second such appointment in his life. But even so! In fact the day was Saturday 10 August 1991 and it was indeed the week before an ultimately glorious Diadora League championship-winning season; a campaign that had the crowds flocking to watch his team. "Sally and I got married in Rowledge Methodist Church and it was a lovely wedding day," he says, at least remembering that much. "We went to Florida for a fortnight on our honeymoon. I had to miss two games and the first was against Carshalton the following Saturday."

Finding out what was happening at home was a different matter in those days when mobile phones were scarce and communication links were further away than just the touch of a button. But thankfully for Chapple, he had a faithful number two who was able to fill him in on the football front. Step forward Colin Lippiatt. "I kept ringing Colin every five minutes," says Chapple. "Because of the time difference I was ringing him at about four in the morning to get him before the game at about twelve o'clock. There I was ringing from the matrimonial bed in the early hours to speak to him and it cost me hundreds of pounds in phone bills. I was desperate to find out how we got on against Carshalton and eventually I found out we won 3-0. Then we won the second game, on the Tuesday, 2-1 against Kingstonian."

It was the beginning of a fantastic time in Chapple's world and when he returned for Woking's third game of the season, a 0-0 draw with Chesham, he was as happy as at any time in his life. the Cards, thanks in no small way to Lippiatt and his encyclopedic knowledge of the local game and its players, had a team to be proud of and they were in the process of becoming the best at Isthmian Premier Division level by a long way. They won the league by eighteen points from their biggest rivals Enfield, despite losing three and drawing two of their last five matches. They were beginning to pull in regular crowds of 1,500, rising to 2,500 as the season wore on, while there was an even bigger appetite from the Woking public for the FA Cup matches.

Chapple's highlight in that season was the league game against Enfield at Kingfield, which his men won 5-0 while demonstrating a scintillating display of attacking football. There were more than 3,000 supporters and it was a brilliant performance. Another to cherish was a 7-1 trouncing of Wivenhoe, and not just because of the amount of goals his side scored. "I remember driving up there in my own car and the traffic was horrendous," says Chapple. "I'd already told Colin the team, and I went to park up behind the goal when the match had already kicked off. As I walked into the ground we scored and I thought to myself I'd got it pretty well-timed to turn up just after we'd got our first goal. When I got to Colin I said to him it was good we were 1-0 up and he said, 'what do you mean 1-0, we're three up.' We'd only been playing for five minutes and I'd missed the first three goals."

Woking ran out to the popular Tina Turner song, *Simply the Best*, that season and although the choice had nothing to do with Chapple, he reveals: "That was our song, Sally and me. It started down the pub when a few of the lads used to play it on the jukebox and they would come to some of the games as well, as our reputation grew."

While Chapple got most of the plaudits for taking Woking into the Conference, he has no hesitation in giving credit to Lippiatt. These were still the days of homegrown players turning out for their local side. There was no such thing as agents, at least not in that standard of football. Nor did players often come from different parts of the country to Kingfield chasing a big contract. "Colin was amazing like that," says Chapple. "He knew far more players than I could ever dream about. Any name you threw at him he'd search it out and if he didn't know, he'd know someone who did. If they didn't know, somebody else would. I'd ring him up in the morning and say 'what about so and so?' Well, he'd speak to the player and be back on the phone to me with the deal done before I'd even finished my cornflakes."

In fact Lippiatt was the man to bring Clive Walker to Kingfield a few seasons later. "Colin went to Slough to see Clive play and when he came back I said 'what do you reckon then Col?' His answer was, 'he was bloody rubbish, but he got a brilliant goal.' So Clive came down for a trial and two weeks later he was in a Woking shirt. That was down to Colin."

Lippiatt was also responsible for another big name player arriving at Kingfield at the start of the 1991/92 championship-winning season. He had known Fulham's number two goalkeeper Laurence Batty since his days as manager at Maidenhead, and Chapple had earmarked the experienced stopper to take over from Tim Read between the sticks. Batty had become a Woking player just after the previous season had ended; a fact not known by many at Kingfield. He met Cards' chairman Ted Hills and Chapple at the Hogs Back Hotel for a chat. "We wanted to seal the deal so we invited Laurence along and we agreed everything," says Chapple. "It was a gentlemen's agreement and while there was nothing signed on the night, everything was done and dusted. Laurence gave his word so we were happy with that. It was a great signing, especially when you get a goalkeeper as they can go on for a few years longer than an outfield player. Chatterbox Laurence I called him. He's a lovely fella and there's not a bad bone in his body. He was also a fantastic keeper."

Batty also got on the scoresheet on occasion, twice in the trouncing of Wivenhoe – once from a drop kick and once from a penalty. He recalls: "Colin Lippiatt was the reason I signed. He'd ring me up every year to see what I was doing. I was at Fulham so it was a step down for me but I'd done a lot of background checks and decided to take the plunge. I didn't know Geoff from Adam at that time. Colin sold me the club but I remember Geoff coming across as a jovial, jolly chap and he obviously wanted to sign me. I joined a very good side and we went on to have great success. Geoff was part of that, even though in nine years I only saw him in a tracksuit twice. And it was a very ill fitting one at that. He wasn't ever on the training ground but what he did well was put jigsaws together and when they were complete people stood back and admired them. What was the secret of his success? I honestly don't know. He was passionate about his football and wanted to win games, although he probably didn't lose any sleep if we lost. Not until later on in his career when it became his livelihood. Basically he got good players in and we just went out and played. He also had continuity with the likes of myself, Darran Hay, Clive Walker and Scott Steele."

Interestingly, Batty reveals there was no game plan as far as he was aware. "I was never given a mandate for whether to throw it out or kick it," he says. "I was just told to play it as I saw it. So no-one knew what we were going to do because we didn't really know ourselves. Geoff would just tell each of us that we were the best in our positions and he told us to go out and prove it. There were no tactics."

With Tim Buzaglo out of the equation for the remainder of the year, George Friel and Steve Milton were the strikers who fired the Cards into the highest level of non-League football. Milton became one of the first men to command a fee when he was recruited from Fulham for £15,000. Dover were later to offer Woking £15,000 for the strike pair but the answer was a resounding no. Buzaglo was "gutted" to miss out on the season but Adie Cowler, Bradley Pratt, Lloyd and Shane Wye, Andy Parr, Trevor Baron, Stewart Mitchell, Dereck Brown and Mark Biggins were all in that superb team. Then there was Batty of course, who achieved the first of his three ambitions in his first season as a Card. "I wanted to win promotion, play at Wembley and play for England," says the lovable keeper. He ended up achieving all three with distinction in his wonderful career with Woking.

Chapple knew just what a great team he had at his disposal at that time and is happy eulogising about the individuals; all of whom have a special place in his heart. "Biggo [Mark Biggins] lit up life with his tremendous displays," he says. "He was a very clever player. Trevor Baron was a Rolls Royce and a lovely fella, while Friel and Milton scored a fantastic amount of goals. But any side I've had has been built around two people who'd go through brick walls. There aren't many clubs going to find them. In our team they were the two Wye brothers. Lloyd was a winner and he'd go through anything for you. He was one of my favourites to be honest. In fact they were both winners all the way through. Shane just wanted to play football. He didn't care if he got sixpence or a shilling. You sat down to talk about a contract with Shane and he'd say, 'just tell me what you think is fair. I ain't here for the money.'" Chapple adds: "They were terrific those two. And we had a great spine to the team. If you've got that down the middle then you're okay. We were by far and away better than anything at that standard."

One player made the difference in terms of what he did to frustrate the opposition and Chapple still chuckles at the role played by Cowler, the inspirational skipper who patrolled the back line as sweeper. "For me Adie Cowler was the key," says Chapple. "Remember this was before the back pass rule came in and there was no-one better at holding the game up than him. The way he sucked people in and nonchalantly strode around was funny really. He'd play it over there and get it back. Then he'd do it again. He'd pass it this way and that and get it back. Then he'd pass it back to Batty. Teams must have been doing their nut when he did that."

Cowler can vouch for the fact they were. "Much later I'd bump into players I didn't know and they all used to say they got really pissed off with me doing it," he says. "We had a wonderful team spirit without any real stars and it was great fun. There was a real confidence about the team which was lovely. Obviously Tim [Buzaglo] and Biggo [Biggins] produced some individual brilliance and Biggo was the key for me. But it was a team of players who gelled and did things at the right times. Each player would also do job after job for each other. I don't think many would have been stars in any other side. It just all came together. But I don't think it was planned as I don't think any manager could have thought four or five years earlier 'this is what I want' and then for it to happen. If Geoff was that good he'd have been manager of Manchester United not Woking. I'm not taking anything away from him because what he put together was exceptional, but I think it was more to do with the fact he was lucky with the players that came to him."

As well as having talented players, Chapple was conscious of needing a good spirited dressing room and he maintains he had that. He also began to bring a new form of togetherness by taking his team to the Hogs Back Hotel for pre-match meals, before they'd all arrive back at the ground together. "Colin and myself used to dip in to our own pockets to take the players up there," he says. "We were starting to get professional. Coming back to the ground at quarter to two on match days, all together with our club blazers on didn't half make you feel good. We did that often."

They were special days for Chapple and Lippiatt and while their team was busy wrapping up the Diadora League title, the thoughts of Conference football began to seep into the consciousness from an early stage. Everybody at the club realised promotion was going to happen.

And that it came about weeks before the season's end came as no surprise to anybody who had seen Woking play.

Although Chapple's initial concern was that of the ground and whether Kingfield was up to scratch in terms of facilities, another consideration came clearly into view and smacked him straight between the eyes. While Kingfield was destined to be deemed fit for the highest tier of non-League football, the question going through Chapple's mind was whether or not his players were up to it. Was the team who had annihilated the opposition on their way to a record-breaking promotion campaign ready for the step up to the Conference? Could the likes of Cowler, short of pace and possibly vulnerable against fitter, stronger players, cope?

Chapple had difficult decisions ahead of him but was not about to let his heart rule his head. He knew he was dealing with men who had brought him unprecedented success. He was aware that those players were desperate to prove they had what it took to adjust to the greater demands. Like a contestant on *Who Wants to be a Millionaire?* Chapple had options. When put on the spot, he chose to ask the audience. In this case various Conference managers who knew the pitfalls of staying with a team that had won promotion. Then he phoned a friend, leaning heaviest on John Still, who had taken Redbridge Forest into the Conference. "I'd been talking to Conference managers all the way through the season but particularly John," Chapple admits. "I had a lot of respect for him. In fact he later applied for the Woking job when I left the first time [1997] and he's the one I'd have picked at the time but they [the Woking board] went for the biggest name in the hat and appointed John McGovern. Anyway I'd been listening to managers telling me certain things and I was trying to take it all on board. They were telling me they had gone into the Conference with the same team and it hadn't worked out, in fact some had failed miserably. By the time they tried to change it, it was too late. I didn't want that to happen to Woking. So I was influenced by that."

Still, who also managed Peterborough United and Maidstone United among others, remains happy with the advice he gave the Woking boss. "I remember those times very, very well," he says. "Like all of us at times, people ask us for not necessarily advice, but to be pointed in the right direction. Geoff and I spoke to each other frequently at that time. He had a very clear idea of what he wanted to do and he wanted to learn what the possible pitfalls might be. We talked it through. I was fortunate in that when I won the Conference it was recognised by Peterborough and I took the opportunity to go and manage there. I would phone people like Harry Redknapp for advice in the same way because being forewarned is forearmed."

If Chapple had it in his mind which way he wanted to go, Still gave him the little shove he was looking for to carry out his convictions. "I'd been in the same situation and it's a hard call when you come to talk about the change in standard and whether you've got players who are good enough to make the step up," Still continues. "You don't want to be halfway through the next season before finding out they're not up to it. I always think the best time to change a team is when it's successful because it's easier to convince players to come to a successful club. No-one wants to come to a club that's struggling and it's easy to get caught in that trap."

After his numerous chats with Still and one or two others, Chapple decided change was the only way and so began the break up of his title-winning team. Out went stalwarts such as Mitchell, Cowler, Andy Russell, Andy Parr, Paul Mulvaney, Bradley Pratt and Nick Collier. Those surviving the cull were Andy Clement, Baron, Brown, Biggins, Buzaglo, Milton and the Wye brothers; although the Wyes missed the first eleven games of the inaugural Conference season because they were playing League football in New Zealand.

Buzaglo, perhaps the man who did most to spark Woking into the force they had eventually become, was to be only a peripheral figure, scoring just two Conference goals – in a 4-0 home rout of Runcorn. "I think the biggest mistake Geoff ever made was dismantling that team and not giving them a chance," says Buzaglo. "He should have given those players a go at it. He got rid of seven or eight when he didn't need to."

Cowler is 100 per cent in agreement and is a man still bearing the scars from the hurt he felt at the time. "Geoff listened to people and was told he should bring in big brawny players but we weren't about that," he says. "We had won the Diarora League by nearly twenty points because of our brand of football and we should have been given a chance. Geoff didn't even ring me to tell me I was out. I heard the news from Chris Kelly who was then Kingstonian manager. Then Geoff got Colin Lippiatt to phone me after I'd already heard. Geoff owed me and the players but he was influenced by external factors." Cowler believes the players brought in as replacements were inferior to those Chapple already had at his disposal at Kingfield. "They were just not as good," he says. "Bringing in people like Trevor Senior and Richard Nugent was nonsense. I can't say we'd have been challenging for the title, but we'd have been top six and we had an arrogance about us, which meant we never feared anyone we played. We played a brand of football that was better than most Conference clubs and we also had tremendous spirit. I would have liked to have played with Kevan Brown though because he was similar to me – except he could run. But Bradley [Pratt], Russ [Russell] and myself could have played in the Conference. I'm not sitting here nearly fifteen years later saying I'm right and Geoff was wrong, but he should have trusted himself and given us a chance. In my eyes he missed an opportunity."

Having ditched the men who had got him into the Conference, it was time for Chapple to bring in some new faces. In came Scott Steele, Senior, Nugent, Brown, Robbie Carroll, Dave Puckett, Mark Fleming and, later on, Colin Fielder and Tim Alexander. The influx of fresh blood brought experience too – although not all would last beyond the season, with Brown, Steele and Fielder the only three to stay the pace beyond Woking's first year in the top flight. "I changed it and took some flak for it from various quarters," says Chapple. "I had to think long and hard because those players who won the League for me did a fantastic job. I remember thinking, 'who the hell am I to stop them playing for Woking?' But I had to put my business head on and I had to do what was right. I couldn't let my heart rule my head, which I'd done many times in football."

Looking back, he has mixed views on it, but maintains he still would have done exactly the same. "I was criticised and justifiably so if you look at our start," he says. "After fourteen games we'd lost nine of them and won just four." Those defeats included a 3-0 home loss to Stafford Rangers on the opening day of the season and his team was then thumped by Stalybridge Celtic, Dagenham, Yeovil and Gateshead. The 5-1 reverse at Dagenham must have been satisfying for Daggers' boss Still. But Chapple doesn't think he was wrong in the action he took. "We finished eighth," he says. "So while I think the criticism towards me was justified in the beginning, I think I was justified in the end. For instance Adie [Cowler] had no real pace and people were telling me how fast the Conference was. It was very difficult but I had to make decisions. Life is full of them. Football is full of them. And opinions as well. It was a soul-searching pack of decisions I made and it hurt me to make them at the time. Because underneath, whatever I'm portrayed to be on the outside, I'll help anybody and I'm a big softie. Not all the signings worked out for me. I remember bringing in Senior, who wasn't 100 per cent fit. I knew he had an injury but thought he'd got over it which proved not to be the case."

With Chapple's revamped squad, crowds of around 1,800 flocked to Kingfied that season and 5,870 turned up to see the FA Cup first round replay defeat at home to Brighton. This after 9,208 had watched the first match at The Goldstone Ground; Shane Wye scoring in the 1-1 draw. In fact the return of the Wyes from down under had done much to save Woking from what could have been a disastrous season, even though the Cards lost their first three games with those two in the side.

The reason for the club's increasing popularity was not because the fans enjoyed watching their team perform in an eye-catching pink kit, it was because of the entertainment value served up by Chapple's new intake. One of those men, Scott 'Jinky' Steele, was destined to go on to have one of the most distinguished of Cards' careers and, but for a personal friend of Chapple by the name of Russell Delaney, he may never have come to Kingfield. Diminutive, skilful and with bags of heart, Steele would become a sensation at Woking, even though his introduction to the club in the summer of 1992 was fraught with complications. "Russell [Delaney] used to be a part time agent and I made it known to him I was looking for a left-sided player," recalls Chapple. "Scott Steele's name came up in conversation, although he was in Scotland playing for Airdrie. Russell did a bit of work and got in touch with Scottie and things moved apace. He was looking to further his career and was obviously wanting to sell himself as he sent me down half a dozen videos. I knew nothing about him at all other than he played for Airdrie reserves. Anyway, I sat down one evening when Sally had gone to bed and I started to look at the videos from somewhere like half nine in the evening. I was still looking at them at seven in the morning because to be honest I hadn't seen him. The reason for that was he was a substitute and I was wondering when it was this fella was going to make an appearance. Eventually he came on for bits and pieces of games while I was drinking coffee after coffee to keep myself awake. I watched him and tried to get my head around the standard. I couldn't afford to get it wrong and here I was watching someone who it seemed couldn't even get a game in Airdrie's reserves. Eventually I'd seen enough of him to learn that the boy could play."

While size isn't everything in many cases, Chapple's first thoughts were that it might well be an issue as far as Steele was concerned, particularly as he had been made very much aware of just how physical the Conference was. "He was no bigger than a milk bottle which worried me a lot," says Chapple. "But things moved on and we invited him down. The big problem I had was I never had a budget to be able to sign him. I was forever trying to sign players and was being told to stop by the committee. To be honest I was giving the committee a bit of grief. I was always trying to find a way round it and sometimes that meant doing it yourself. In the case of Scottie it was a case of giving him a little bit of cash in his hand and providing him with digs. It wasn't much cash, we're probably talking less than £100 a week. But giving him somewhere to live for two years was the only way and that's what we did."

There was another issue, as Chapple explains: "Getting him down to us was one thing but because he was a player moving from Scotland to England there was another hurdle. Airdrie wanted £22,000 for a player who couldn't even get in their reserves. Negotiations were ongoing and all sorts of things were threatened but we settled for a fee of £8,000. To be honest we were never going to get away with it scot-free."

Chapple had already made the decision on where Steele would live. He had gone with his belief that sometimes you just have to get on and do things yourself. So he became the provider, allowing the young Scot to live under his roof with him and Sally. "I welcomed Scottie to my house and his parents came down to check me over," he says. "They were lovely people and came with his brother all the way down from Scotland as they all wanted to make sure he was happy where he was and the environment he was in. So in he came for two years. I liked him a lot. He was a well-mannered boy. We were only training twice a week at that time and during the days he would be out playing golf. He was a bloody good golfer I believe."

Chapple soon began to realise it was not just a player staying at his home but a young man growing up. "Not only did I welcome Scottie to my house, it was a case of welcoming his harem of girlfriends," he recalls. "I met two or three of them, nice young ladies they were. Then like all

Scotsmen he liked a drink. He pebble-dashed my walls once or twice and muggins here had to get rid of it. They were just little things but all part of him growing up. There was something there though and the boy did me proud. I honestly feel that we got our money's worth as a football club out of him. He was a character and not short of an opinion. He was very forthright but with me he was fine and he gave me total respect, like a son. I've seen him rear up at people and there's a few at Woking Football Club he doesn't like, but I can only speak well of him and it was a real pleasure to be invited to his wedding in 2005. He didn't forget and the irony was that he had his reception at Farnham Castle which he used to drive past to go and play golf when he was living with me."

As a twenty-year-old becoming disillusioned at Airdrie, Steele grabbed the chance to come south of the border and doesn't regret a moment. "Geoff looked after me when I came down and I'll always thank him for that," says the Scot. "I was living upstairs on the top floor of their town house and was there for about two years, which was probably a year too long. In hindsight I'm not sure Sally was that happy about me staying after their daughter Lucy was born. There were sleepless nights with a baby in the house but that's life and to be honest I probably kept Geoff and Sally up more than the baby did. We never really saw each other too much when I was there but when we did we'd always have a laugh. Geoff loved a wind-up and was always laughing. That's the greatest thing about him and what makes him such a great character, although Sally used to go off her head at times at his wind-ups. The other thing I remember is Geoff never wanting to drink when there was anyone around. But every cupboard in his house was filled with whisky. I brought him a lovely bottle down from Scotland once and it was gone within a week. I never saw him drink it though. He used to drink pints of coke but I reckon they were pints of whisky with a dash of coke. Living with Geoff, I used to get loads of stick off the players and they used to call me things like 'son of Geoff'. But it was a good base for me until I left and rented a place in Woking because eventually that's where all my mates were."

So, the time leading up to Chapple's first year as a top level non-League manager had been fulfilling on many fronts and littered with decisions that would alter the landscape of his personal life and that at Woking Football Club. Now, years later, Chapple still wonders about what might have been. Although he would have done the same again, there is a nagging thought in his mind that refuses to move aside. Just how would that Diadora championship-winning team have fared in the Conference? "In hindsight I'd have loved to have seen how that team might have done," he admits. "But I'd made the decision and was happy with it."

The irony is that, later in his career, and at another club, he would make the mistake of sticking with a tried and tested side rather than break it up as he did at Woking. Then, at Kingstonian, he had known exactly what needed to be done but it was another occasion when he let his heart rule his head. It was a conclusion that would come back to haunt him. And of all places, he made a snap judgement at his very own theatre of dreams – Wembley Stadium.

6

Tunnel Vision

'Immortality is a long shot but somebody has to be the first'
– Whoopi Goldberg

One might have expected that a manager who had been to Wembley five times and won on each occasion would be egotistical and absorbed in self importance. The fact that this phenomenal winning accomplishment should come in a magical seven-year spell would surely inflate that person's self glorification to bursting point. Well Geoff Chapple may well still have an expansive waistline, but it has nothing to do with egotism or conceit straining to find an outlet from his heavy frame. He will always retain his effervescent nature but he remains humbled by his own achievements, preferring to shy away from the limelight rather than take centre stage.

In fact, for the first three wins at Wembley, with Woking, he says there was no secret formula to the success, nothing that made him think anything other than that he was a lucky man to have experienced what he did. He had super footballers in his teams of course and doesn't flinch when admitting that having so many of them over the years had a major bearing on why he had tasted more good times than most.

Sir Alex Ferguson knew exactly what he was saying when he told reporters they were asking the wrong man when enquiring what it was like to win at Wembley. Explaining just how his non-League counterpart managed to triumph there so often would have been beyond the Manchester United icon though. If Chapple and those who were close to him couldn't work it out, then how could Sir Alex be expected to?

Chapple's fixation with the old Wembley Stadium can be traced back to his teenage years, when, as a lad aged fourteen, he wrote a school essay saying he wanted to play there. It was almost as if he was destined to get to the Twin Towers in some form. His first calling came at the end of his second season as a Conference manager, a term which hadn't started well. The Cards won just once in eight games, with three defeats and two draws in the opening five. "I remember we lost 5-0 at Dover in the fourth game and a voice in my ear said, 'what the bloody hell do we do now,'" says Chapple. "That someone was Colin Lippiatt. I just told him we weren't going to do anything other than sit tight. Eventually we turned it around."

Woking actually finished third in the Conference at the end of that 1993/94 season and beat Sutton United to win the Surrey Senior Cup. But it was in the FA Trophy where Chapple's men showed their star quality. On the way to the final they beat Bashley, Dagenham & Redbridge, Bromsgrove and Billingham Synthonia, over two matches, before a two-legged semi-final against Enfield, which went to a replay played at Wycombe Wanderers.

The Enfield clashes bring back vivid memories for Chapple, not least because of his rivalry with one of two particular adversaries he had at that time, Enfield boss George Borg. "I can remember the build up to the final that year very well because I'd had some run-ins with George because he was slating us," says Chapple. "George always had good sides but he was one of the few managers who never beat me in any match. At home to Enfield in the semi-final first leg, we drew 1-1 and, right at the start, Graham Roberts put one in his own net. The second leg was 0-0. I always remember their player Martin St Hilaire who was one of the quickest things I've ever seen on legs. Thankfully for us he missed a sitter in the very last minute of extra time."

Chapple was far from happy with some of the things said by Borg prior to the replay between the sides at Adams Park. "It was at that time that successful clubs were setting up call lines and I set one up at Woking," he says. "On a good month it was bringing in £1,500. It was one that I could actually input from home. Well Enfield had one too and George had gone on his and said some very nasty things about Woking. One of those was about us being good at having people sent off. Well we all know what happened at Wycombe in that third game. Not only did we win 3-0, but they were the team that went down to ten men not us. I remember Graham Roberts stepping onto our coach afterwards and shaking everybody's hands. That was nice as it was the second time he'd had a rough deal from me after what happened at West Brom."

Borg was obviously bitter about defeat in the semi-final of such a major competition but looking back he has nothing but admiration for Chapple. "Geoff's been a great manager and he knew how to build a solid, strong side that brought him success," he says. "When people talk about great non-League managers who should have gone on to manage in the Football League, Geoff's name crops up. His system was difficult to break down and when Enfield played Woking they were always tough games, in the League fixtures and in the cups. Geoff was one of the first men to play the five system [at the back] and it worked for him. Let's be fair, the man's a legend in his own right and no-one can hold anything to his record. Maybe he wasn't the most gifted of coaches but his man-management skills were second to none."

Borg's relationship with Chapple was not without its problems though, and the former Aldershot Town boss admits: "We had some rows and one in particular when Geoff gave me Carl Hoddle on loan when he was injured. Carl only played one game for us. I slaughtered Geoff for that and went absolutely ballistic at him but we made up over a meal. To be honest I thought he was the loveliest man I ever met. He was so funny too. But I could have taken a leaf out of his book because where I'm bullish, Geoff was very diplomatic and came across so well when he was on the telly."

Having beaten Borg in that semi-final replay, Chapple remembers what a poignant night it had become in his life as his sentiments got the better of him. "My own personal emotions on that night, well they were just that, very personal," he says. "I don't think there are many people at Woking who knew what happened. I got off the coach when we got back to Woking and my first thoughts were of my parents. They didn't even know I was Woking manager as they died in 1980 and 1981. For some unknown reason I just had to go up to where they had lived. Living right out in the sticks as they did it was up dirt tracks and different roads. Bearing in mind I'd been away from there for twenty years or more and my parents had died thirteen and fourteen years before, it had been a long time since I'd been. I just sat outside that house, at quarter to two in the morning, and booed my eyes out. It was so emotional. I just got overcome and I had to get rid of the grief by myself. I sat there and had a bloody good cry and even now when I think about it I get choked up."

He arrived home about three o'clock in the morning, still high on adrenaline. And as he was awake he thought he might as well update the

Cards' call line. "Normally I didn't write anything down, I just used to ad-lib it," he says. "Then if I didn't like it I'd do it again. I don't remember the details but I know I started this particular one by saying 'the dream is now a reality; Woking are going to Wembley.' Then I carried it on." Chapple's message had touched many people, or at least those who could afford to ring at 60p a minute, and he adds: "I was just in the right frame of mind to do it because I was speaking from the heart. I couldn't believe I was going to Wembley and it was fantastic."

One fan who was listening was Lynn Corbett, a founder member of the Woking FC Supporters' Club and someone who devoted a great deal of time in helping out where she could at Kingfield. Chapple recalls Lynn ringing him later in the day to tell him she'd cried after hearing his words. She remembers those halcyon days with affection. "Geoff was a big part of my life back then and it was no surprise he moved me to tears as there is nothing I wouldn't have done for him," she says. "The club staged a semi-pro international one night just twenty-four hours after we played Farnborough Town at home in a Conference match. There we were, Geoff, my friend Sue Cook and me, spending the afternoon before the international sweeping up that whole stadium to make sure it was ready for the evening. I remember Geoff standing there with his broom as we all had a cup of tea, chatting about this and that and reminiscing about old times. That's how it was with us. I met my husband Adrian at Woking and we became very good friends with Geoff. We were big fans of the club and we didn't think twice about getting on the long coach trips to see Woking play. In the first three years of the Conference we never missed a game and would have gone anywhere to support Geoff and Colin [Lippiatt]. We took all the success for granted then and I don't care what anybody says, those days will never be recreated. Not a day goes by when I don't think about those times."

Reaching Wembley had been Chapple's dream from childhood and now he had realised it. Like everybody in the Woking camp on the day of the final against Runcorn, the thing he remembers most was the weather. "It pissed down with rain and any other game would have been called off," he says. "I have watched the video many times. We won 2-1 and for the two goals we got from Dereck Brown and Darran Hay, their keeper was at fault. It was a marvellous occasion. The club was getting very big and at that time we were fast becoming, and I still maintain we did become, the biggest non-League club in the world in terms of stature and profile. So I was unbelievably proud to lead Woking out that first time and people have often asked me what was I thinking about as I walked out of the tunnel and across the pitch. Well I was thinking about my parents mainly. I was obviously proud looking at the sea of red and white in the crowd. And that would have been enough for me, to do that just once in my lifetime. I've said it many times – I could have sat inside Wembley when it was empty and got a thrill out of it. Little did I imagine that I'd be coming back another four times."

The tears flowed after the game as Chapple and his team attended the post match reception in a bar underneath the Twin Towers. "To be honest I wasn't a great one for receptions," he says. "I just liked to celebrate quietly. I'm funny like that. I'd rather drive off into the country somewhere and be on my own. I don't have to be with a crowd of people. But in the bar Phil Ledger [football director] came up to me and asked me if I had a minute. He put his arm on my shoulder and we walked away across the room to an empty corner. As we walked over there he broke down and cried and said, 'you don't know what this means to me.'" Another committee member at the time, Paul Elmer, known for his rather dour demeanour, also looked affected by the occasion, something that stuck with Chapple as it was such a rare moment to see him like that.

Who would have thought that a year later Chapple and his players would be making the same pilgrimage along the A40 and on to the Hangar Lane Gyratory System for another May Day cup final on a hallowed patch of grass in north London. While getting there in 1994 had been hard enough, during the following season Woking were to take on some of the biggest names in non-League football, on the way to the final. What's more, they beat them.

Chesham United, the Cards' first round opponents, might not have been among what was an elite band, but they were the exception, because Cheltenham Town, Stevenage Borough, Macclesfield Town and Rushden & Diamonds certainly were. The 3-0 win at Stevenage was special, as was the one goal triumph at Macclesfield – never an easy trip at that time.

Being paired with Rushden in the semi-final was a major task. They were managed by Roger Ashby, who was later to hand over the reins to Brian Talbot, who was to complete his mission of taking Diamonds into the Football League on the back of chairman Max Griggs' money. Griggs, who owned Doc Martens footwear, was not a large man in stature but he made a big impression on Chapple. "It was lovely to meet this fella called Max Griggs and what a real gentleman he was," says Chapple. "We played Rushden away and lost 1-0 and then there we were at Kingfield, before the new stand had been built, beating them 2-0 with goals from Kevin Rattray and Clive Walker. What I remember most about that game is afterwards when Max went into his own dressing room. The way he was building that club up it was obviously going to be the best non-League club we'd ever seen. He must have been absolutely gutted to lose but he walked in and said to his players, 'never mind lads, there's always next year.' I thought what a wonderful thing to say. He was so calm about it. He was a lovely man."

Just for good measure, Woking were to play Kidderminster Harriers in the final; a club who had already forged links with the Cards following the epic FA Cup battles in the 1990/91 season. "That was another special one because it was Kidderminster," says Chapple. "The second time you do try and take it in a bit more. People were telling me it goes like a flash and they were right. I remember on the way to Wembley we were nearly there and we turned this corner. All of a sudden we came right up behind the Kidderminster coach and under the tunnel we went. I loved going into that tunnel. It was tremendously exciting."

Chapple was good at keeping his feelings under wraps and he maintains that nobody knew whether he was nervous or calm. What he does know is that the second Wembley occasion was a better day all round. Two good footballing sides locked horns on a pitch like a billiard table and Woking got off to the perfect start with a sensational first-minute goal from Scott Steele, one of the quickest in Wembley's history. "Scottie scored that cracker then they fought back with a goal, before Colin Fielder scored in extra time which was a dramatic moment," says Chapple. "There were scenes of great emotion again and there I was with my second medal. I was elated but at the same time disappointed for their manager Graham Allner because I had a lot of time for him. That night I didn't want to leave the stadium. I could have slept there all night. To get one medal was marvellous but to get a second was special."

Allner, who had won the FA Trophy with Kidderminster in 1987 after a replay at The Hawthorns, adds: "I think we were two minutes away from the end of extra time when Fielder scored. The replay would have been at The Hawthorns again and I had visions of it all happening for us a second time. But we lost, although I would say that whichever team won in the games between us there was never any animosity. There was a real respect there for each other and the two clubs have remained friendly since the first time we played each other in 1990."

For Fielder, who had signed from Slough Town just a few games into the 1992/93 season, it was a big moment and he feels pride at contributing to Chapple's unprecedented success. But few will know he had crossed paths with Chapple as early as 1980 as a fledgling teenager. "I was about fourteen and used to follow Alton Town home and away when Geoff was player-manager," says the hugely likeable Fielder. "I used to live down the road from the ground and I was there when they won the Hampshire Senior Cup at The Dell. Geoff was a good player even then, strong and a good passer. Later on in life I nearly signed for him in the late 1980s but I went to Farnborough because they were in a higher league at the time. Then when I heard Woking had come in for me, when I was at Slough, I said 'yes' before I'd even spoken to Geoff. I knew I wanted to play for him. Scoring that goal at Wembley in 1995 was what you dreamed of as a schoolboy. I was in two minds whether to go up for the corner but I normally did so up I went. In fact just before that I'd been wondering whether I'd be able to get time off work for the replay." A few seconds later, having bulged the net with his header at the tunnel end, Fielder wiped away any concerns about that potential problem.

Steele had also been happy to help justify the faith shown in him by Chapple three years before. But he doesn't recall ever getting a 'well done' from the boss. "He wasn't the kind of guy who'd say that," says the Scot. "In fact I can't remember him saying that to anybody. He'd cuddle you though. Or look at you and give you the best smile in the world. Then you knew you'd done well. We were a good side and he always knew his best team. Luckily I was in it. He'd always have a great speech before games and would build every player up by telling them how good they were. And he'd just let you go and play, there was no pressure. In fact it was a bit of a culture shock when I first came to Woking because up in Scotland we used to have a manager who'd want to hang us from the coat pegs if we lost. With Geoff, nobody ever said anything and I was in a state of shock about that for a long, long time. We didn't lose many though because he'd got great players in and played them in their best positions. They were brilliant times."

1996 was a year when Woking did not get to the FA Trophy final. For Chapple it was rather like being a student enjoying a gap year. Two years on, one year off, and another year on to come to complete the course. But he was now big news, especially where this particular cup was concerned. And so on the day Macclesfield Town played Northwich Victoria in front of the competition's lowest final attendance in history – less than 9,000 – the Woking boss was there again. Only this time it was as a Sky TV pundit. "Because I did the commentary I didn't really miss out in a way," he says.

He enjoyed the different perspective of viewing a Trophy final from way up high on the other side of the pitch to the players' benches, but as he sat viewing proceedings, Woking's exit from the competition at the first hurdle was still fresh in his mind. The defeat had come away to Carshalton Athletic on a beach masquerading as a football pitch. Their manager, a certain Fred Callaghan, was all too aware of Woking's penchant for free-flowing attacking football and the Colston Avenue surface was liberally sprinkled with sand. "I must admit having seen the pitch earlier on in the week, I was surprised that much sand was necessary," Chapple had said diplomatically at the time.

In the following 1996/97 season he was back in more familiar territory for the final; in front of the Royal Box in his usual position, directing operations from the bench alongside the other two parts to the famous trio, Lippiatt and physio Barry Kimber. Incredibly, Chapple had made it to his third final in four seasons and this time it had been at the expense of another old adversary, Paul Fairclough, at the semi-final stage.

It was hated rivals Stevenage Borough who stood in the way of Woking and another Wembley visit. Fairclough had at his disposal the likes of Efetober Sodje, Barry Hayles, Dave Venables, Corey Browne and Gary Crawshaw, all huge players for a club who were locked in a battle for supremacy with Woking both on the pitch and on the terraces. But Chapple thought Fairclough took matters too far. "It was the Enfield scenario all over again, only this time with Paul Fairclough and not George Borg," he says. "I had a lot of respect for Paul but he would never let the name Woking be mentioned at their club, which was bordering on the ridiculous I thought. We both had good sides. They gave us one or two hidings and we did the same."

The stakes were massive as the two clubs collided at Kingfield for the first leg of that famous last-four clash. Robin Taylor's early thunderbolt was enough to separate the two sides in Woking's favour on the day, but in a titanic second meeting at Broadhall Way seven days later, Woking were a goal down within a minute through Hayles. Then Kevan Brown was sent off in the first half to leave Woking down to ten men and really up against it. But they rallied, and Darran Hay scored in extra time to make it 2-1 overall. However, Crawshaw lobbed Batty to take the clash into a third date at Watford's Vicarage Road.

"For me the Stevenage away game was all about one player," says Chapple. "That man was Lloyd Wye. When we went down to ten men he played out of his skin. He always gave 100 per cent but he dragged another 20 per cent in from somewhere. He was a man-mountain and it was a fantastic performance. In fact the whole team showed a tremendous will to win." Wye admits it was his best game by a mile – for any club at any level. And yet he only played because Steve Foster was suspended. "I was the serial sub that year because Geoff preferred Robin Taylor," says Wye. "But I thought I'd be in for the Stevenage game when Fossie was suspended and I was desperate to play in it because it was a massive game against Stevenage, who I hated. In fact I still do now! I wasn't particularly match-fit and at 5ft 9in tall, I knew I'd be playing at centre half against Neil Trebble who was 6ft 3in. But there was no pressure on me as I knew it would be a one-off game. The game plan was to keep it tight early on so that Stevenage would get frustrated. But Barry Hayles scored after only fifty seconds so that went out of the window. We knew then we were involved in a massive cup tie and it would be backs to the wall stuff. And that's how it turned out, although that was largely down to Browny being sent off."

Wye was magnificent alongside Terry Howard and says: "Every challenge I made I won and every pass I hit went to one of our players. But the only reason my performance stood out was because it was our defence who were doing all the work. I didn't need extra time because I was absolutely knackered. And I still think that if I hadn't gone off with cramp we'd have won the tie in that game."

Man of the match in that semi-final second leg in what Chapple claims was the defender's best game for the club in more than 500 appearances, Wye was dropped to the bench as Woking looked to make it to a third final in four years at Vicarage Road. "I think everybody in the dressing room knew that Geoff was concerned about how I would react to being dropped," says Wye. "When he named the team you could sense all eyes were on me but the dressing rooms are L-shaped at Watford and Geoff made sure he was just out of sight so there was no eye contact between us. Whether that was deliberate I don't know. I do remember him sticking his head around the corner to see how I'd taken it. I just kept my head down. There was tension in the dressing room and the players were all shocked and surprised I'd been left out. But I wasn't."

Chapple confirms: "I was a great one for picking my best XI and as much as I liked Lloyd, that's what I did. Uriah Rennie was the ref that night and I remember arriving at Watford and walking out on to the pitch. And there were the Stevenage players all dressed in flash suits, strutting their stuff as if they were the kings of England. They really did think they were the bees' knees. They had also gone to a Conference dinner dressed in white suits, even the women. It looked smart but they'd have been better off among the opera singers at the Albert Hall."

Chapple's men won 2-1 with goals from Clive Walker and Andy Ellis. Wye made it on as a sub, although he reveals: "It was 2-0 to us and Stevenage were coming back at us. Then Geoff wanted to put me on. He didn't think I was good enough to start but he thought I was good enough to go on and help keep it tight. So I stayed warming up at the other end of the pitch for as long as I could. I couldn't change the game and felt, purely selfishly, there was nothing for me to gain by going on as the team looked comfortable. But it turned out alright and when I ran on my brother Shane came over soon after, shook my hand and said, 'congratulations on your 500th appearance.' I was so nervous about the match and had so many things going around in my mind I hadn't heard the tannoy announcer and had no idea I'd reached that milestone."

After the match, Chapple got involved in something he had never done before. "Our players had noticed the Boro players giving it some before the start of the match," he says. "So after we'd won and had finished celebrating with our fans, all our players banged on their dressing room door as we went past it. I don't think that went down too well." Bearing in mind Stevenage boss Fairclough's admission that he and his players were devastated by the result, it was hardly surprising.

With other players rested after that semi-final showdown, Wye got to play some League games, knowing full well he wouldn't make the starting XI for the Trophy final, even though he was among the substitutes. "I respected Geoff for that," he says. "There were never any selection surprises with him because he wasn't a tinkerer and knew his best XI. I still respect him now and the only thing I didn't like was finding out from Basingstoke manager Ernie Howe that I was being released by Woking.

Geoff couldn't even tell me first. I felt after more than 500 games for the club I deserved better than that."

For his part Chapple doesn't ever recall telling Howe and says: "I suppose Ernie might have rung to ask what my plans were for the following season but whether it was Colin [Lippiatt] or me who said something to him I don't know. I can't speak for Colin, but I don't recall saying anything specific to Ernie about Lloyd. And if anything was said, it would have been confidential between two managers."

With Wye playing his part in reaching Wembley, Chapple enjoyed that moment at Watford as his team had played superbly, Clive Walker the catalyst for all that was good about them. "They were terrific times and the games against Stevenage were fantastic," says former Chelsea, Sunderland and Brighton star Walker; now a pundit for Sky TV. "I'm still suffering today from those times in the mid-1990s as a matter of fact. Whenever I go to Stevenage the fans there still give me a hard time. I can go to any ground in the country and there is generally a bit of respect, but at Stevenage I still get verbal abuse. It must be to do with the fact we played them about ten times back then and we usually beat them. I think we won eight and drew one in my time. So I can understand why they don't like me but although life seems to have stood still for them, I've moved on."

Despite the big games Walker was involved in with Chelsea and Sunderland, that semi-final at Watford still gives him a warm feeling. "It was huge for both clubs and one of those semi-finals which always stands out," he adds. "We got some great results against Stevenage and that was one of them."

Slowly, after FA Trophy semi-final victory number three began to sink in, the emotions came to the fore again for Chapple. "There I was thinking, 'God, three times'. The bigger shocks were to come later with Kingstonian but I was still pretty amazed to have made it to Wembley a third time."

Chapple left the Sky summarising to another pundit and set about the task of overcoming Dagenham & Redbridge, complete with their adopted West Ham United fans who swelled the Daggers' number on another exciting day for all concerned at Kingfield. "We basically set out to pass them off the pitch," says Chapple. "There weren't many teams to match us at that and even though we hadn't scored and it stayed 0-0, I kept thinking we were doing all the right things. They had a bloke sent off and I remember saying to the players after ninety minutes, 'don't get flustered because there's no score and we're passing the ball well and making them run all over the park.' We made the pitch big. In fact we passed almost to the point of rubbing the leather off the ball. And the pitch suited us of course. There wasn't a weed in the place. When you go up there on the invitational days you see eight people there with their own mowers, doing their own little bit in the ground. There was no better place for pass and move football."

Once again Hay was the man for the big occasion, scoring a wonderful header in extra time to seal a one-goal victory and give Chapple his third triumph under the famous Twin Towers. "I took Kidderminster to Wembley three times and only won it once – in 1987," says Chapple's old pal Allner. "I was proud of that record so for Geoff to do what he did at Woking and then go on to virtually repeat it at another club was quite amazing."

Chapple knew that what he had just accomplished was incredible to say the least. "I did think it was special," he says. "But I didn't think I was fated or that someone was smiling on me particularly. People always ask me which one of the three was the best and it has to be the first simply because it was the first. To get two medals was marvellous, to get a third was really special."

But while things had been nothing but a success story on the pitch, with the FA Trophy win complemented by a fifth place league finish and an FA Cup third round draw at Coventry, there were rumours of unrest in the dressing room and plans were afoot to unseat Phil Ledger as Woking chairman. "That last Trophy win was achieved under a cloud," recalls Chris Dyke, journalist with the *Surrey Advertiser*. "Player discontent was rife, with disillusionment at Chapple's methods and those of coach Colin Lippiatt leading to outpourings in our paper. Woking still had a formidable team though and their extra time win against the Daggers illustrated their inner spirit which so often carried them through when it most mattered."

Fielder, who only made nine starts in Chapple's final season, has his own theory on what may have hindered Chapple's desire to keep a happy dressing room. "Geoff was a man of few words and sometimes he wasn't the best man manager in that if there was a problem he'd go shopping or not come in and let Colin [Lippiatt] deal with it," he says. "But he wasn't afraid to admit he'd made a mistake on a player and get another one in. Of course you need a budget to do that and everyone knows if you gave him a tenner he'd spend fifty. But then there's that question. Do you want a successful side or not? It worked for Geoff and that's how he did it. Signing Clive Walker was pivotal because everyone thought he had only come to Woking for the money. But he never missed a game or even a training session, although he certainly missed a tackle! And if you asked him, Clive would say he had four of the best years of his career at Woking. We all looked up to Clive and some of the team wouldn't have been half the players they were if it wasn't for him in the side. He gave us all belief. And Geoff was the one who took a gamble on him. I have nothing but admiration for him as a manager and what he achieved."

As for the boardroom shenanigans, Chapple says: "What was going on behind the scenes was awful. People were ringing up and trying to win votes on the phone for the meeting that was coming up. Jon Davies [committee member] was one of the ones accumulating votes and getting the members to vote for him. Derek Powell [committee member] was one who got voted off and I know that upset him."

Powell wasn't the only man to feel aggrieved. There had hardly been time to allow the champagne and euphoria of Wembley to wash over him, when Chapple was dramatically ousted himself. Not directly of course, as he resigned from his position. But a vote of no confidence had been shown in him by certain people and it was enough to make him realise that he had suddenly become yesterday's man. It was time to move on.

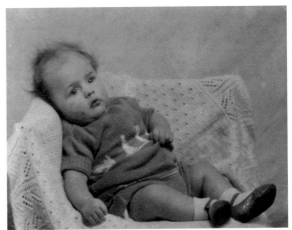

Clockwise from top left:

1. With his mother, Maisie, in his beloved Farnham.

2. Geoff aged four and a half months.

3. At St Andrew's infant school, Farnham, aged five.

4. Bill Chapple, far left, at the Sussex & Dorking Brick Co.

5. Farnham Town FC, the early years. Geoff is front row, centre.

6. Geoff in action for Farnham Town early in his career.

7. Farnham Town FC in the 1960s. Geoff is front row, second from right.

8. Lining up with Heath United FC. Geoff is back row, second from right.

9. Receiving the Hampshire Cup at The Dell with Alton Town (photo courtesy of *Hampshire Chronicle* Newspaper Group).

10. Alton Town FC. Geoff is front row, third from left (photo courtesy of *Hampshire Chronicle* Newspaper Group).

Left: 11. As a player with Guildford & Dorking United.

Above: 12. The 1970 version of that great Alton Town team. Geoff is front row, third from left.

Right: 13. Geoff's first wife, Linda.

Below: 14. Scoring the winning goal for Alton in the Hampshire Senior Cup final, early 1970s (photo courtesy of *Hampshire Chronicle* Newspaper Group).

15. Receiving Manager of the Month award with Windsor & Eton in 1981.

16. Jimmy Butters and family, prominent members of Farnham Town FC.

17. With HRH the Duke of Edinburgh, patron of Windsor & Eton FC, in 1981.

Above left: 18. Starting out as a manager at Windsor.

Above right: 19. With lifelong friend George Priest.

Below: 20. Woking FC team 1985/86, Geoff's first full season in charge at Kingfield. Author Clive Youlton is back row, fifth from right (photo courtesy of the *Surrey Advertiser*).

21. Early Woking action, with Trevor Baron and guest keeper Peter Bonetti (photo courtesy of the *Surrey Advertiser*).

Above left: 22. With Sally on his wedding day, 10 August 1991.

Above right: 23. Addressing a dinner after Wembley 1995, with daughter Lucy in tow.

Left: 24. Goodison Park before kick-off at Woking's FA Cup fourth round clash in 1991.

Below: 25. The Cards in action against Everton (photo courtesy of John Shore).

Above left: 26. With former Woking mayor, Les Pescod.

Above right: 27. Receiving the Conference runners-up trophy from league chairman, Bill King, in 1995.

Top right: 28. Geoff gets a big hug from his seven-year-old daughter.

29. At a pre-Wembley visit, 1994.

30. Woking FC Committee in the mid-1990s.

31. Leading team out at Wembley alongside Kidderminster's Graham Allner in 1995 (photo courtesy of the *Surrey Advertiser*).

32. Triumphant Woking trio, physio Barry Kimber, Geoff and Colin Lippiatt (photo courtesy of the *Surrey Herald*).

33. At an end-of-season Conference dinner with trophy haul.

Right: 34. Voted Manager of the Year in 1994/95.

Below: 35. With former Everton and Scotland manager Walter Smith at Goodison Park.

36. With Frank Lampard senior, West Ham's assistant manager, at a testimonial in 1995 against the Hammers.

Left: 37. With Cards' talisman Clive Walker and 'Captain Marvel', Kevan Brown.

Below: 38. As boss of a Woking all-star XI with Westfield FC's manager John Cassidy (centre) and chairman Steve Perkins (photo courtesy of Bill Beminster).

Above: 39. Sharing a joke with World Cup winner Nobby Stiles.

Below left: 40. All smiles with Dennis Rofe, Geoff's assistant at Kingstonian in 1997/98.

Below right: 41. Preparing the Kingstonian mascot in the Wembley tunnel (photo courtesy of Eric Marsh).

Above: 42. The Kingstonian hordes at Wembley Stadium in 1999 (photo courtesy of Garry Letts).

Right: 43. Giving last-minute instructions to Ks' substitute Delton Francis at Wembley in 1999 (photo courtesy of Keith Clayton).

44. The team at Wembley in 1999 (photo courtesy of Garry Letts).

45. On the way to Trophy win number five in 2000 (photo courtesy of Darren C. Thomas).

46. With Dave Leworthy at the striker's testimonial.

47. With Ian McDonald before the 2000 final (photo courtesy of Ian Morsman).

48. With former Chelsea manager Ruud Gullit (photo courtesy of Chelsea FC).

Above: 49. With assistant Glenn Cockerill on his return to Woking in 2001.

Left: 50. Geoff and Colin Lippiatt, back together again (photo courtesy of The Swift Partnership, Mike Swift).

51. In his van at Farnham Town FC in March 2006.

52. With his Farnham Town FC working party colleagues in March 2006.

7

Ever Decreasing Circles

'If I were two-faced why would I be wearing this one?'
– Abraham Lincoln

June 1997 was to become another pivotal month in Chapple's life and managerial career. Not only did he quit Woking, his marriage to Sally was about to spiral downwards along the path to acrimonious divorce. Both events took their toll on him. On the one hand he secured a contract to satisfy his new-found need for security, even though it was Kingstonian, not Woking, who provided it. On the other, the longer hours away from home and the need to get stuck into a new job began to have a bearing on Sally's happiness.

Chapple had never had a formal employment contract at Woking and found his desire for one increased when Sally returned home from a pre-term meeting at Rowledge School, near Farnham, prior to his daughter Lucy starting there. Coming up to five years old, Lucy was about to enter the next phase of her development. But that meant expenditure. "I only did it for them," says Chapple. "Sally went down to the school one night and when she came back she told me how we needed to get this and this and this. All I said was, 'bloody hell I'd better get myself a contract.' However, Woking were saying sorry but they couldn't give me anything in writing." The writing was on the wall as far as his tenure at Kingfield was concerned.

Then came the call from Jon Davies, who was about to be installed as the Cards' new chairman. "Colin and I went to see Jon," recalls Chapple. "At the time we were planning for the following season player-wise but chairman at the time Phil Ledger wasn't able to agree anything because Jon was taking over. So anything we wanted had to be agreed through him. There had been a lot going on behind the scenes and I was well aware that Phil [Ledger] was having his nose put out of joint. But he wasn't getting involved in ringing people for votes; some were, but Phil's philosophy was if people wanted to vote for him they would because he was Woking through and through. Anyway we walked straight into Jon's house and his opening remark shook Colin and me rigid. He said to us, 'right, what are you doing then, are you staying or going?' Well, Colin and me looked at each other perplexed as if to say, 'what was that all about?' I think Jon was pretty thick with Clive Walker at the time but I don't know for sure. And I think he probably wanted Clive to take over as manager. He may even have promised him the manager's job after I'd gone. But when I did leave, the powers that be saw to it that he never got it."

Davies believes to this day that Chapple – who he refers to as Geoffrey – and Lippiatt had already lined up a move away from Kingfield, but he made a pledge with Chapple at the time he would never go into details about their discussions together. "Woking FC was going through an enormous period of change and the cup runs we had were covering over the cracks," says Davies, who was subjected to unwarranted personal abuse during his time in the chair. "We needed to go to that extra level," he adds. "Geoffrey wanted a contract but he had never had one before and the committee were not in a position to let him have one then. I remember saying to Geoffrey in one of our meetings together, 'if you win the league you won't have to worry as you'll be made freeman of Woking.'"

It was clear from the subsequent appointment of ex-Nottingham Forest skipper John McGovern that Woking wanted an extra professionalism they felt Chapple could not supply, while they perceived his team to be an aging one. Davies wanted youth to be given a chance as part of his vision for the club's future and although he maintains he didn't want Chapple to leave, he didn't really do a great deal to keep him. Regardless of that he adds: "They were good times and whatever magic Geoffrey had he made it work. He had good, experienced players at the club and you can't knock his achievements."

Contrary to suggestions that Chapple and Lippiatt had lined up a move away from Kingfield long before that fateful meeting with Davies, Chapple maintains to this day that the Kingstonian offer came out of the blue. In actual fact the directors at Kingsmeadow did not think for one minute that Chapple was about to become available. But a phone call at home from one of them was about to change his life. It was Terry Weir and, unwittingly at first, he became the man who was instrumental in taking Chapple to Kingstonian in what was a shock move for all concerned. In fact Weir's recollection of events flies in the face of Davies' notion that Chapple and Lippiatt had long since done a deal to move from Woking. If they had, it was certainly not with Kingstonian. "I actually rang Geoff to apologise," said Weir. "Our manager at the time was Graham Westley and I had to get rid of him. In a meeting with Graham, it came up in conversation he'd been tapping up certain Woking players which I wasn't happy about. So after Graham had left the club I rang Geoff to apologise. It started off as that conversation but of course we were now looking for a new manager. Rather tongue in cheek I asked him whether he would be interested and I expected him to say 'no'. But he said, 'as it happens I'm not too happy with some of the things going on down at Woking and wouldn't mind having a chat.' It progressed from there."

Weir had got his teeth into something tasty and like an *I'm a Celebrity Get me out of Here* contestant who'd stumbled across a three-course meal in the jungle, he was not about to let it go. "At first I told him I wasn't interested in moving," recalls Chapple. "Terry accepted that I was in love with Woking and that I didn't want to leave. But me and my big mouth. I was just about to put the phone down and I said, 'you never know, Woking might leave me one day.'" That sentence had been all the encouragement Weir needed and the wheels were set in motion.

Chapple, not under contract and therefore free to talk to any club, was a salesman by trade and what followed might have come out of his own school of giving the punter all the right flannel. "They planned it brilliantly," he says. "I met them and they turned up with all the papers and showed me a million pound balance sheet. They laid it all on the line. They told me they'd give me £40,000 to get a side together, which they did. And they said they'd increase my wages, which they did. Well I needed a contract and with the position I was in, it was an attractive proposition. They wanted a decision from me quickly because they had targeted two people, George Borg and me. Chris Kelly and one or two other Ks directors wanted Borg. The majority wanted me."

A meeting was arranged at the Hogs Back Hotel on a Thursday night, when Chapple would let Weir's colleagues know his decision on whether or not he wanted to become Kingstonian manager. But first he brought forward a further meeting with Davies, for lunchtime on the same day. "Jon Davies didn't make me leave Woking," says Chapple. "But Lucy was starting school and I needed security. Kingstonian were putting me under pressure because they wanted to let George [Borg] know one way or the other. So I brought the meeting forward with Jon. When I arrived at 1p.m. he was already in the hotel sitting down. So I walked up, sat next to him and said, 'any change your end Mr Chairman?' 'None whatsover,' he said."

From that moment Chapple knew he was going. "When he said that to me I replied, 'in that case, you leave me with no alternative but to leave Woking Football Club.' He said, 'okay I'll notify the press and the committee accordingly.' Then we shook hands because we never fell out. And that was that. I was leaving Woking but I didn't feel as low as I might have done because I had something to go to."

Sally, rather than be happy with the job security her husband was about to gain, found she couldn't cope with him leaving Kingfield. "My missus loved Woking the same as I did," says Chapple. "Very shortly after that she was desperately upset. I remember Phil Davies [committee member] seeing the state Sally was in one day. She was crying her eyes out. She'd worked in the kitchen at Kingfield, had pictures of Lucy in a Woking kit, that sort of thing. The point is I left for her but I can't say it worked out for the best to be honest. When I was at Kingston I was away from home a lot more because I had to build a side there. Looking back it was probably the start of where it all went wrong."

Chapple is bitter about the split with Sally, although they are still civil to each other for the sake of Lucy. "It was one of the old boys at Farnham who was doing some work, fitting some bedroom furniture in our house," he recalls. "I must have been out and he said to Sally that his son had always held a candle for her. They'd been in the same class at school. So she left me for him and they're still together now."

The bitterness comes from the financial situation he found himself in once the parting of the ways became final. "I shouldn't have a mort-gage at my age," he says. "I lost everything. I had to buy Sally and Lucy a house but we went to mediation, which was a more friendly way of doing things. There I was in the room watching the blackboard and the chalk and this lady saying, 'yes Sally, you'll need that and Lucy you'll need that.' It went on and on and then it was, 'oh and Geoff, there's that left, that's yours.' So now here I am living in a shit-hole. I could have a

How Geoff's departure was reported in the *News & Mail*.

nice garage and a nice garden but I spend all my time doing someone else's garden, Farnham Football Club's." There are far worse places to live than Chapple's but he believes he should be in better accommodation.

Despite the personal heartache, Chapple's season at Woking had been an incredible one by anybody's standards and at the start there had been nothing to suggest that Woking would not continue to be part of his life. Prior to the start of that 1996/97 season at Woking, the Cards had come tantalisingly close to gaining promotion to the Football League on a couple of occasions. There was little doubt they had an excellent side, but there were some supporters who were beginning to think Chapple wasn't getting enough consistently good results in the bread and butter of the Conference.

However, he maintains there was never any pressure on him to take the club to the next level of the football pyramid. "The only pressure I was under was the pressure I put on myself," he says. "The Football League is where we all wanted to go and we felt we could do it. We'd been getting so close, so much so that we might have gone up in second place when the winners [Macclesfield] were not allowed to. I did feel sorry for Macclesfield. The authorities were allowing Chester City to play their games on their ground but when Macclesfield won promotion it was considered unfit.

So it was okay for Chester to play Football League matches there but not Macclesfield. It was scandalous. So was not allowing Kidderminster to go up when they won it. Stevenage Borough should have gone up at the time they came top too. But Woking didn't put me under pressure. They knew it was something I wanted and they wanted it as well. We were ready on the pitch. But we weren't ready to go into the Football League off it at any of those times. The club just wasn't geared to go."

Not many managers would lose their job after finishing fifth in the League, winning the FA Trophy for a third time in four years and becoming the first non-League side to hold a Premiership club on their own ground in the FA Cup. Technically, Chapple didn't lose his position but then again what he had achieved was not considered worthy of a contract offer, which defies belief.

The FA Cup run was special. The first round saw Woking host Millwall, top of the third tier in English football at the time. Woking Police may not have been too enamoured with the draw, given The Lions' reputation, but it represented a real test for Chapple's men against a side managed by former Northern Ireland international, Jimmy Nichol. "It was a very cold night," recalls Chapple. "And it was Martin Tyler's first commentary on Woking for Sky TV. We got a great start and I've watched it many times on video. We drew 2-2 and the one I do like is our first goal. We get a quick free-kick. Clive Walker does a shuffle down the right and sends over a pinpoint cross, because he was probably the best crosser in football at the time, and Steve Foster came in and headed it in to a beautiful white net. It looked lovely. At the time Millwall were flying high and it was a good test of how far we'd come. We were pretty relaxed for the replay to be quite honest. I certainly was. We'd gone there thinking that we'd got a draw at home and the boys had done me proud. At that time I had a team who were full of surprises. It was a point in my managerial career when I knew, nine times out of ten, we were going to do pretty well. I'm not going to say win. But there were so many people in that team, in that jigsaw, that could do different things. I knew somebody was going to run through a brick wall. I knew somebody was going to provide quality. I knew somebody was going to score a goal. There were pieces of the whole team that made it bloody near perfect for that time and at the level we were at."

For that reason, the Cards' boss was unfazed by the New Den, a wonderful ground with an intimidating atmosphere. "I remember walking out on to the pitch at Millwall," he says. "It was an empty stadium and a nice pitch. I was looking around the ground and I had a feel and a buzz of adrenalin going through me. I knew Millwall were going to be in for a game. I've seen Jimmy Nichol's interview since, the one he did before the match on Sky. When they went back into the studio the pundits were saying, 'he's not totally confident about this game tonight.' That's because he'd seen enough of us in the first game to know how good we were."

After the home team had missed a good chance in the opening minute, Walker scored what proved to be the winner and Woking moved comfortably into the next round. Cambridge United were next, a side who topped the old Third Division (now League Two) at the time with the likes of Dion Dublin in their side. Roy McFarland was manager at The Abbey Stadium and he had been working as a pundit on Sky when Woking had beaten Millwall. Not only had he thought Millwall would win, he never gave Woking a prayer. "There he was saying we wouldn't beat Millwall and there we were going up to beat his side too," says Chapple. "Walker lobbed the first goal and that was sweet. Whether he meant it or not it was a bloody good goal. Cambridge had beaten us twice before in the cup so that was a sweet moment."

So on to Coventry City in the third round, a match that was postponed twice and in the end didn't get played until the day of the fourth round. "It was a marvellous draw," says Chapple. "It didn't matter who it was just as long as they were in the Premiership."

It was time for him to do some homework on The Sky Blues. "I kept going to Coventry to watch them play," he says. "I went to see them play Sunderland, Man United and Newcastle, who were managed by Kevin Keegan at the time. I went to that game with the club secretary Sue Day as she was Keegan mad. As the Newcastle bus drove in to the ground Mark Lawrenson was at the front and he waved at me. And when Coventry played Man United the team coach pulled up and I remember Alex Ferguson getting off the coach and walking straight down the car park towards me and saying 'hello Geoff'. He didn't need to do that in the car park before the game. That was a nice touch."

It was at Coventry on one of his scouting missions that he bumped into another famous manager, with his not quite so well-known side-kick. "Normally I'd go unannounced and stand there with my cap on," says Chapple. "That's how I used to do my scouting. But I'd gone into the scouts' room to have a biscuit and a cup of coffee and I saw these two fellas there and I said 'bloody hell what are you two doing here?' It was Glenn Hoddle and John Gorman. Glenn said, 'hello Geoff, how are you?' and told me that Highfield Road was one of the few grounds in the country where they don't let the England manager in the board-room. So I had a cup of tea with them. In fact I sat with Glenn during the game. He kept pointing things out to me. He'd say, 'did you see this and did you see that?' He was very approachable and he was pointing out the weaknesses for me. So that was good."

The Woking playing contingent did not travel to the first postponed match with Coventry, but Chapple and one or two of his colleagues made the trip anyway – to sign Justin Jackson from Morecambe. The striker cost £35,000 and many saw it as a hasty decision in the wake of the failure to sign fans' loan favourite Guiliano Grazioli. Chapple refutes the notion. "It never even crossed my mind. We did nearly sign Grazioli but Bill Sutton [finance director] wasn't happy with it and said that he'd arrange the finance then resign. He hadn't been happy with us signing Darran Hay either and I think he left the club for a time then. We'd agreed a fee of around £18,000 for Grazioli. We'd met the boy and everything was agreed but it fell through. Then we signed Jackson."

Chapple remembers the day of the second scheduled clash at Highfield Road. Fog had hampered the journey of just about every Woking fan on a Tuesday night that couldn't have been worse driving weather. Visibility was so bad it was difficult to see more than twenty yards. But several hundred fans did make the trip and the irony was that around ten miles from Coventry the fog suddenly cleared. One of the groups travelling up was a coach party from the Woking printing firm, Unwins, the company where Cards' chairman Phil Ledger worked.

Chapple takes up the story. "I remember Phil being on his phone and being told the Unwins coach had broken down and would not make it to the ground," he says. "Apparently, someone on their coach called out, 'don't worry Phil Ledger will fix it.' Anyway, the game was called off later and Phil rang the fans on the coach to tell them." Ledger adds: "I told this chap that we'd cancelled the game and there was a big cheer in the background. When I told him the news I heard him say to everyone else on the coach, 'there you are, I told you Phil would fix it.'"

While the cheers rang out on Unwins' coach, both Chapple and Sky Blues' boss Gordon Strachan were gobsmacked by referee Gerald Ashby's decision to call the game off. "There were loads of supporters in the ground, including Sally," says Chapple. "Strachan came across and shook my hand on the pitch, which looked excellent to be honest. But there was a hard patch in the middle. It was perfectly playable in my view and Strachan didn't seem that bothered. Then Gordon asked me 'what's he doing?' and I told him the referee wasn't sure about whether we should play. Then Gerald came across and said, 'gentlemen, it's 7p.m., and no, it's not going to happen because the centre of the pitch is rock hard and it's dangerous.' I must admit he was a charming fella but he didn't do himself any favours that night. It worked out well for us though."

Finally the game was played on fourth round day and a 16,000 plus crowd saw a dramatic last minute leveller from Steve Thompson cancel out a goal from Coventry's Eoin Jess. The unthinkable had happened again. Chapple admitted to having a good feeling about the game beforehand. "We got ourselves pumped up for it and the adrenalin was flowing," he says. "Again I had this little bit of expectancy because I knew we could play no matter who we played against. I knew that no-one was going to steamroll us, although you do get the odd one like when Dagenham & Redbridge beat us 8-1 at Kingfield in between the two Enfield FA Trophy semi-finals in 1994. But here we were against Coventry with Steve Foster having a magnificent game, while Shane Wye was out of this world. When Thommo's goal went in there were almighty scenes and I remember Geraint Hughes on BBC Southern Counties Radio going absolutely bananas when we equalised. He screamed 'they've scored, they've scored' and the last thing I remember him saying was 'what a performance'. It was brilliant because we knew we had a replay."

An unfortunate own goal from Foster proved Coventry's winner in that second encounter after Scott Steele had equalised Noel Whelan's opener. But the night will stick in Chapple's memory because of what happened after the final whistle. "As the players walked off Laurence Batty must have said something to one of their players which was heard by others," he says. "I think he said something like, 'if that's the Premiership then you're relegated.' Gary McAllister took offence and said something like he's worth every penny of his £20,000 a week. Then the next thing I know, he and Strachan come bursting in to our dressing room trying to get at Laurence. Thankfully he saw sense but only after a few people had dived in between the pair of them to stop it getting nasty.

My motto is win with glory and lose with dignity no matter how hurt you are and maybe both players were at fault. It was sad for us because we ran Coventry very close that night."

It was the end of another exciting chapter in Chapple's bulging portfolio of FA Cup adventures, while in the FA Trophy, the Wembley finale with Woking beating Dagenham 1-0 to win their third FA Trophy in four years, was another superb achievement. Not enough though, as it turned out, to earn Chapple the contract he so wanted. There had been talk of him having lost the dressing room, with unrest in the Woking camp spiralling out of control since Jackson's arrival. There were some big characters at the club with Walker, Steele and Batty in particular never short of an opinion. Walker and Batty were thought to have disliked the expensive centre forward and are said to have almost come to blows with Jackson at different times. "I was aware that something wasn't right because there had been a set to with Justin [Jackson] and one of our players after the Wembley appearance," says Chapple. "Woking Borough Council had kindly made arrangements for players to go and celebrate as a group on their own and I believe Laurence [Batty] and Jackson nearly came to blows. I didn't have a problem with Justin. But I got him lodgings at Richard Shaw's [former Premiership footballer] mum's house and I think he gave her some problems. So I'm not surprised there was some trouble. It was brought to my attention afterwards that players had refused to pass the ball to him which although it wasn't totally apparent in the games, showed there was certainly a dislike of him by certain players."

One of the dominant figures in the dressing room, Batty, confirms the spirit among the players was not good. "We had some good players who were brought in but the team morale wasn't always there," he says. "Up at Southport one time Geoff accused the players of having cliques but I stood up and told him there wasn't anyone in the dressing room I didn't like. It was just different."

Chapple maintains he had no intention to leave Woking and was busy planning recruitment for the following season until that meeting with new chairman Davies confirmed the doubts in his mind about whether he was still wanted at Kingfield. John Still, a big ally to Chapple in the non-League game, believes that the fact that Chapple never made it in to the Football League should not be allowed to blight his record. "I can't speak for the directors of Woking at the time but what I would say is have they had the same level of success since? Have Kingstonian had the same level of success? The questions answer themselves. What Geoff did in the FA Trophy was incredible. It hadn't been done before and it won't be done again. His sides always played good football and he had the right philosophy. The fact he never won the Conference should not detract from how successful he was. Success is relative. If you are Manchester United, Arsenal, Chelsea or even Liverpool, success is winning the Premiership, or a cup or the Champions League. If you're West Brom it's just staying in the Premiership. Listen, a manager can win a cup if it's his year. But not five times in seven years. That just doesn't happen. It is a fantastic, incredible sequence of results in a major competition. It's like a club such as Charlton winning the FA Cup five times in the same time-span."

Still also tosses aside suggestions that Chapple was lucky. "People talk about Geoff being lucky," he says. "Well I don't believe in luck. You can be lucky once, but not five times. The harder you work the luckier you get and even if Geoff didn't go near the training ground once, and I'm not saying he didn't, whatever way it was that he did it was the right way for him. If you think of Brian Clough and how he did his job, nobody would run a club like he did again but that's what worked for him. I'm sorry Geoff never had a crack in the Football League because he'd have done a fantastic job."

Batty, who went on to manage Ryman League Walton & Hersham, believes Chapple had managed at the highest level he could. "I'm not privy to what the Woking directors were thinking but from what the players' gathered, they did think Geoff's past record was fantastic but the question was could he take the club up a level? I think he was at the level he could handle. The higher you go in football the more you need to sort any problems with players out on the training ground. If a player is on a two-year contract and not playing well, you can't just drop him and freeze him out hoping that he goes of his own accord, then get someone else in. That's what Geoff tried to do. And he was able to do that lower down, but the higher you go clubs can't afford to do it. You can't keep acquiring players and then drop them as a punishment for not performing, unless they're not on contracts. You have to try and improve that person and get him playing well again by working with him on the training ground. Geoff didn't do that and while you can't knock him as a man or for what he achieved, I think the directors wanted someone who could."

So Chapple was on his way out of Woking and to this day maintains that if he had drawn up a list of clubs close to his heart at that time, Kingstonian would have been right at the bottom of the pile. As it turned out they were the only club interested. They offered him an increased salary and made such a big play for him he could only ever feel wanted.

The directors at Ks reacted as if they had won the lottery when Chapple went back to the Hog's Back Hotel to sign his contract just hours after meeting Jon Davies at the same venue. And contrary to thoughts that Kingstonian chief executive Kelly would have preferred Borg, he maintains he was as delighted as any of his colleagues with Chapple's appointment. "I had known George [Borg] for a while and had a closer relationship with him," says Kelly, the former 'Leatherhead Lip'. I just didn't know Geoff and to be honest I never dreamed we'd get him. Terry [Weir] had made it his mission to get him but he'd just won the FA Trophy with Woking so for him to come to us was staggering. Of course he came at a price because nothing came cheap with Geoff and with the players he brought in. His man management skills were unique and while he wasn't a coach, he was very charismatic and managed to get players in that gelled quickly. While it went sour in the end, he was a brilliant manager for three of his seasons with us and no-one can take that away from him."

Chapple remembers the feeling when he put pen to paper for his new club. "There I was in the same room I had been in earlier in the day with Jon Davies, just about to sign my new deal when the phone rang," he says. "One of the directors said, 'if that's Woking tell them we want £100,000 for him.'"

Weir was in the Far East on the day Chapple joined the Ks but he had been the man to set the ball rolling. "It was obviously a huge wrench for Geoff to leave Woking," said Weir. "But I think he felt let down by people there even though in my opinion he was the best there was in non-League football at the time. It was just a throwaway line I gave him and when he gave me a glimmer of hope I pursued him relentlessly. Some of our directors fancied Geoff, although Chris Kelly wasn't one of them because he thought he'd have his nose put out of joint. But we couldn't believe that Geoff agreed to come. He was the best thing to happen in the history of Kingstonian Football Club."

Although the wrench of leaving Woking would not sink in for weeks, this sort of adulation was at least a comfort to Chapple. So too was the support of loyal friends he left behind at Kingfield; Eric and Pauline Jackson, Brian Westen and Mike Smith, all of whom helped during what was a stressful time for him. All four did not want him to leave. There were others too who had become close allies to Chapple, namely kit man Ron Rawlings, head groundsman Colin Galliford and Brian Finn, ex-Cards' skipper from Chapple's playing days. "I learned a lot from Colin while Ron was a diamond who later helped me at Farnham," says Chapple. "Brian was someone I had huge respect for and he was always around when I needed help and advice."

Chapple was now Kingstonian's boss though, and going to the Conference dinner a couple of weeks later as the manager of a Ryman Premier Division club was, by his own admission, a strange experience. So were the clashes with his old team where Kingstonian invariably had the upper hand against the Cards. "We left Woking standing at times but that wasn't something I was proud of," he says. "We played them once in the Surrey Senior Cup. When we scored someone from Woking Borough Council jumped out of his seat to shout out 'yes'. He completely forgot where he was!"

While he had dropped a level in the football pyramid, Chapple did get to return to the Conference within a year of leaving it. But the fact it was with a club other than his beloved Woking was something he would take a long time to get his head around.

8

Special Ks

'Being complimented always embarrasses me. I always feel they have not said enough' – Mark Twain

For him it was a typical Monday morning. Geoff Chapple, full-time football manager, left his Farnham home and made his way to the Shepherd and Flock roundabout outside the town centre before taking the A31 towards Guildford. He was on his way to work. He made his way past the Hogs Back Hotel, scene of many an emotional moment over the years, and continued on to the A3 before meandering up past the Burpham junction and on towards Send. He had been treading the same path for thirteen years and could have done the journey in his sleep. Only this time there was a difference. This time he didn't take the Potters Lane turning and make his way along Send Barns Lane to Woking and, despite the enormous urge to ease the steering wheel left and veer up the slip road, he maintained his path towards London. This time he was heading for Kingston and Kingstonian FC.

In the coming weeks he was to find that he would turn off left on two or three occasions purely out of habit. By his own admission, driving to start life at a different club felt weird. He was nervous, excited and like any other person on their first day in a new job, wondering what it would be like when he walked in to a new environment for the first time. "I felt very strange," he says. "It was a culture shock. Not to say that Kingstonian didn't make me welcome. On the day I started there were people there who treated me as if I was some sort of royalty. I walked in and a couple of guys there said, 'I can't believe you're here.'" In fairness, neither could Chapple. But there he was and he knew he had better get used to it.

Most people might have spent a bit of time finding their feet in a new position but Chapple didn't waste a second in setting about his immediate task, that of building a team. He had a budget of £40,000 burning a hole in his pocket and he began to sign players he knew would be suitable for a Ryman Premier Division title challenge.

One player, Wycombe's Matt Crossley, was all set to join Woking until Chapple told him he had been appointed manager of Kingstonian. "Once Matt knew I was going to Kingston he said, 'that's fine, wherever you go I'll go,' so that was my captain sorted out," says Chapple.

"I sat down with a piece of paper and had a look at what I had. Obviously people like Eddie Akuamoah were still going to be some use to me. Scott Corbett was another. Then I signed big Terry Evans who was massive. Wayne Brown was pretty near his peak at the time. He'd been around a bit and was a big stocky lad, a firefighter from London. Over the period of a few days we signed a few and I remember Chris Kelly was looking at the players thinking 'what are we signing?' because they were all man-mountains. But I knew what I needed. Whatever league you are in you need to have players who can play in the next league up, just to be able to get into it. That's the theory I worked on."

Brown had rung Chapple and said he wanted to play for him. Geoff Pitcher was already there. Another key midfield player, Gary Patterson, would soon follow. "Slowly we were putting a jigsaw together," says Chapple. "And without even seeing them play I thought I had a decent side."

In his first week at Kingstonian, club secretary Bill McNully, part of the furniture at the club since the year dot, knocked on Chapple's door. "He asked me whether I had a minute and then said he'd been at the club a long time and before he retired he'd like a shot at the Conference," Chapple adds. "I reminded him I had just got my feet under the table and told him to give me a chance."

Colin Lippiatt had joined Chapple at Kingstonian, the double act inseparable at that time. And the boss tried to make it a threesome when he asked Barry Kimber, the third member of the tightly knit group he had at Woking, to join him as Kingstonian's physio. But the genial injury guru could not be torn from a club he had been associated with since 1974. "Geoff did invite me to Kingstonian," says the amiable Kimber. "But I'd have only been going there to do a job and Woking were far more than that to me. They were my club." "I appreciated Barry's decision," says Chapple. "The three of us were a team but Woking was where he felt he belonged."

Lippiatt stayed for the first part of the season but Chapple recalls it was not long before he was looking for another coach. "I think Colin thought we weren't going anywhere at the time and he came in to the office one training night and told me he had a problem. When I asked him what it was he told me he was leaving to go to Yeovil, who were in the Conference, to work with Graham Roberts. I told him in that case I was the one with the problem, not him. But it was amicable and I didn't want to stop him doing what he wanted to do. But I was stuck then as I needed someone quickly."

Chapple maintains the man he brought in following Lippiatt's departure was one of the main reasons Kingstonian won promotion that season. Ex-Southampton and Leicester City defender Dennis Rofe was out of work and, through one of his many contacts, Chapple rang him up, offered him a job after an away match at Yeading and appointed him the following day after Rofe had slept on the offer. He was destined to re-join Southampton at the end of the season when he was replaced at the Ks by Ian McDonald, but he had done a fine job. "Dennis was a coach and a half," says Chapple. "A real character, a disciplinarian and good fun with it. He was a great boy to have around."

Apart from the change of coach halfway through the season, that first year in charge of Kingstonian was a bit of a blur for Chapple. He does recall battling it out with Boreham Wood for the Isthmian League championship and winning promotion at Oxford City, even though that seemed an unlikely scenario given where the club were around Christmas time.

It had taken a while for the side to bed down and Chapple recalls. "We made a few changes early doors and I remember we went to Dulwich Hamlet on Boxing Day and were losing 1-0. We had a keeper on loan and he bent down to pick this ball up and it went straight through his hands. That was a bad day and it left us about twelve points behind the leaders. But after that game we never looked back. We took the League by storm. Boreham Wood were up there, they were the ones we were worried about. We went there in the League and they absolutely battered us but we won 1-0 thanks to David Leworthy. How we won that game I'll never know. Sometimes you think somebody is smiling on you. They certainly were then."

Kingstonian Supporters' Club chairman Colin Deadman believes Chapple's motivational skills had a huge hand in the excellent run of results that followed. "I remember when a loyal fan, Jack Goodchild, died," he says. "The road next to the stadium was later named after him. Well his obituary went in the *Surrey Comet* and in the first team talk after Christmas Geoff put the obituary up on the dressing room wall for the players to see. We did really well from that day on."

If any two players were the engine room of a team then Pitcher and Patterson were two such men. Pick out any double act you like, Morecambe and Wise, Punch and Judy or Pinky and Perky and Kingstonian's dynamic duo were up there alongside them. "Patto was all action while Pitch was the craft, class and guile," says Chapple with a broad grin. "They are smashing blokes too."

Pitcher loved his time at Kingstonian and says: "It's funny because in the four years I was there I only ever saw Geoff on the training ground twice. Basically he had a good group of players and we had a great team spirit. Geoff had a real knack of getting players and he did an unbelievable job considering Kingstonian were relatively small at that time. I won five trophies there so it was an enjoyable time for me."

Chapple adds: "We had a great team. Steve Farrelly was a massive presence in goal and the team was built on solid defence. And we tried to play football. We had a bit of pace up front. Then we had workaholics in midfield, the class of Pitcher, while Colin Luckett was strong at left back. Patto was everywhere and not much got past our back three. And some of the tackles I saw Terry Evans make were frightening."

The title-winning display at Oxford City sparked emotional scenes at the final whistle. That was when Chapple saw grown men cry again; something he had not experienced since seeing Woking director Phil Ledger blub his heart out at Wembley in 1994. Kingstonian's directors had been around a long time and the realisation of a dream, Conference football at Kingsmeadow, had come to fruition. No wonder they could not hold their emotions in check.

On the Monday after the championship had been clinched, Chapple received a knock on his door back at base. It was McNully again. He had shed a few tears two days earlier and was asking Chapple for another two minutes of his time. "He said it had been brilliant winning the league but he had another matter to bring to my attention," says Chapple. "I didn't have a clue what he was going to say but then he told me he'd always wanted to go to Wembley and asked whether that could be arranged. I told him to go and sling his hook."

McNully, who had put in around thirty years of service at the club, was later to get his wish, not once but twice. "I was on the brink of retirement and Geoff came at just the right time for me," he says. "His whole attitude was so laid back I'd never seen anything like it. We played Bristol City in the cup later on in his time and he approached it as if he was going off to play bingo. He never panicked and his ability to get on with people was special. You could have filled a stadium with the names he had in his contacts book and he brought some wonderful players together at that time."

The first thing that cropped up in Chapple's mind following Kingstonian's promotion to the Conference was that he would be on his way back to Kingfield to face Woking as an opposition manager at some stage. He never imagined it would happen after just a single season in charge of his new club. He had a five-year plan at Kingsmeadow and had fully expected it to take two or three seasons to make the break-through back into non-League's elite. Kingstonian were a big name with a long and distinguished history, albeit mainly at their previous ground in Richmond Road. But they were also a smallish club, and that Chapple had already added to the roll of honour surprised even him. Little did he know then that he was about to tread a familiar path in his second season at the club – one involving the A40 into London.

There were more than 2,000 fans at Kingstonian's historic first Conference encounter, goals from Leworthy and Delton Francis enough to beat Hereford United 2-0. Chapple admits his feelings towards the club were changing, not least because of the supporters and he thoroughly enjoyed his return to the top flight of non-League football as Kingstonian more than held their own. They managed the double over Doncaster Rovers and took four points off Yeovil Town and Stevenage Borough. Some low points accompanied the highs, notably two 5-1 drubbings against Rushden & Diamonds and Dover Athletic.

Then there were the two matches against his old friends at Woking. An inauspicious 0-0 draw on Boxing Day at home was followed by a 1-0 win at Kingfield on 1 January, thanks to Lee Boylan's goal. It was not a result he particularly enjoyed. "I don't think I ever lost against Woking but it was strange going back," he says. "I wasn't looking forward to it at all and the only time I'd been in the away dressing room at Kingfield was when I'd painted it. I knew we'd go back and give them a game. Lee got the goal. He was a lad they said I would never get away from West Ham.

When the opportunity came along I snatched it with both hands. I had sold Gavin Holligan to the Hammers and when I was up there I noticed Lee. As time went on we got him." Boylan started just four Conference matches for Ks in that season though, with Leworthy and Akuamoah the chief strike force.

But it was in the cups – the Ks competing in an incredible twenty-three ties during 1998/99 – and one cup in particular, where Chapple's team shone. It was FA Trophy time again, a competition that had become synonymous with a certain grey-haired, overweight but genial man who had already walked out at Wembley three times and emerged as a winner on each occasion. His dominance of the famous old trophy was about to scale new heights.

Wins against Kettering Town, Gloucester City and Whyteleafe set up a fifth round tie against Yeovil Town at Kingsmeadow. It was one of the toughest draws Ks could have been handed, but a Simon Stewart goal in the eighty-ninth minute took them through to a quarter-final at Northwich Victoria.

David Piper, Yeovil's right full-back, later revealed to Chapple something the boss had been oblivious to on the day. "I saw Dave at Scottie Steele's wedding in 2005," says Chapple. "He told me when we played them some of our lads kept telling the Yeovil players during the game that they'd never win. Pitcher and Patterson were the main ones. Every time a Yeovil player got near them one of those two would say, 'you'll never beat us.' When one of the Yeovil players eventually asked what they were talking about they just said: 'You won't beat us because it's Chapple's trophy.'" Pitcher says: "I don't remember saying it but then it was the sort of thing we would have done." As it turned out it was not an idle boast.

Having beaten Northwich 2-0, Kingstonian could have drawn St Albans or Forest Green Rovers in the semi-final. Instead they got FA Trophy holders and Conference winners Cheltenham Town, who were hell bent on securing a famous double. "You don't get much tougher than drawing the holders and champions," says Chapple. "It wasn't a draw that inspired me because nobody beat them. I knew I had players that could upset the form book, but Cheltenham were pretty near your modern-day Chelsea in non-League terms."

Steve Cotterill's side had also done the double over Chapple's men in the league. Everybody expected the Gloucestershire side to win the tie over two legs. The first match at Kingsmeadow ended in a 2-2 draw,

IT'S JUST GOT TO BE WOKING

Interview by Richard Spiller

Says former Cards legend and Shots fan Geoff Chapple on the tie everyone is talking about

HERO at Woking, lifelong fan of Aldershot – no wonder Geoff Chapple has divided loyalties for tomorrow's FA Cup fourth qualifying round tie.

The big man will be supervising his Kingstonian side in their game against St Albans but would be inhuman were his mind not to wander off to The Rec.

"I know every inch of the pitch there," said Chapple, an apprentice straight from school in the days when the Shots rode comfortably in the Football League, long before their slide started to extinction and had to start again as non-league Aldershot Town.

Habit

"My dad started it by taking me there when I was four and then, when I was 16, I had a couple of seasons in the days Dave Smith was manager and Jimmy Sirrell the coach.

"Their result is still the first one I look for, out of habit - more than anything."

Chapple did not make a first-team appearance for the club and moved onto a well-travelled non-league career, leading in turn to management.

He will have to perform miracles at Kingstonian for his time at Woking not to be regarded as the apotheosis of his footballing life.

Finishing runners-up in the Conference twice running was a superb achievement but it was those heady FA Cup runs which will always be most closely associated with Chapple, the heroic defeats by Everton and Coventry matched with

● Hands on: Geoff Chapple's name became synonymous with the FA Cup

● Hands up: Proud Chapple was a triumphant Woking manager but he never hid his love of Aldershot

A feature in *The Advertiser*.

with Stewart and Pitcher weighing in with the goals. The second clash, a week later, saw Chapple more intent on not letting some of his old Woking friends down than on ensuring his team were up for the biggest game of their lives. "I remember it was a horrible day and we went to a hotel before the game," he says. "I had invited some friends along and had arranged to meet them there. They were en route and I had tickets for them. They came in two cars but they apparently drove straight past the hotel and kept going."

Plans were altered via mobile phone and Chapple arranged to meet them in the car park at Cheltenham's Whaddon Road ground. The Kingstonian team coach pulled in about 1.30p.m. and in the players went for their cup of tea and to mill around. Chapple was with them in the dressing room but he slipped out the back door and back into the car park. "I'm standing around at twenty to two and really I needed to be in the dressing room," he says. "This was the FA Trophy semi-finals. People saw me out there waiting around and wondered what I was doing." 'Is there a player late?' was the general thought from Ks fans as they looked quizzically at their team's boss. Chapple made his way back to the dressing room, still with tickets in hand, and gave his team talk. Well, he thought he ought to. "I've gone in there and it was a pretty easy team talk really as the prize was Wembley," he says. "I asked the players how badly they wanted it, told them it was achievable on a lovely surface and told them we had some big time players. I also said it was theirs if they wanted it."

They wanted it, there was no question of that, but all Chapple wanted was to offload the complementary tickets that were becoming a nuisance. Again he trotted out to the car park. "I must have been standing there until about twenty-five minutes to kick off," he says. "I don't let people down. I had their tickets and I thought all I can do now is to get them passed on. It was crazy really. It's something that would never happen. I eventually saw one of my friends coming through the turnstile. I had a right go at him effing and blinding. He told me because they'd driven past the hotel they'd gone on to get some fish and chips before coming to the ground." The Ks boss was not amused. At least not at the time.

Thankfully Chapple could now concentrate on the football and he was not to be disappointed. "We performed out of our skins and played them off the park really," he says. "We had to withstand a bit of pressure because they were a good side with good players." Goals from Crossley, Leworthy and Patterson saw Cheltenham humbled 3-1 on their own turf.

Perversely, Chapple never saw the end of the match. Once Patterson's goal had sealed the tie in the eighty-seventh minute, he had stood up and quietly slipped away down the tunnel to the dressing room. "It was a good five minutes before the whistle blew," he says. "I walked in because I couldn't believe it was happening to me again. I just wanted to be on my own. Nobody had noticed me come in and I sat in the dressing room and made myself a cup of tea. I heard all the commotion at the end. And I went back out to do some interviews after five or ten minutes. I just felt numb. I was thinking, 'promotion last year and now I'm going back

The back page of the *Kingston Star* after the semi-final second leg.

to Wembley again'. I'd taken a lot out of myself. Players can run off their adrenalin but managers can't. On Saturday nights I was absolutely knackered. The best thing I could have done then was get my tracksuit on and go for a five-mile run. Then I might have felt better." Remembering his physical condition and his dislike of tracksuits he laughs and adds: "Actually I probably wouldn't have made it out of the gate."

Cheltenham were not best pleased to have missed out on their expected Wembley date but Kingstonian's players were beside themselves with pride, and rightly so. But Chapple never felt what was happening to him was fate. "If I was fated I'd have been a manager in the Football

League," he declares. "I was just blessed with players who could play football, and I mean football. We passed Cheltenham off the pitch, we really did."

Beating the Robins so emphatically was a wonderful achievement for a club that had just one Conference season behind them. For Chapple it meant a fourth trek around the Hangar Lane Gyratory and on to the famous twin towers of Wembley Stadium. It was getting to be rather like an annual pilgrimage for him and this time Forest Green Rovers stood in his way of a fourth win after they had disposed of Garry Hill's St Albans.

The run-up to the match had its stresses, not all of them related to matters on the pitch. Something that left a bad taste in the mouth at the time and still annoys Chapple to this day concerned the kit for Wembley. "You have to wear Umbro walk out tops at Wembley," he explains. "Basically we didn't and the Conference fined us £1,200. I'd ordered them quite a long time before and they arrived at my house, with no logos on, about two to three weeks prior to the match. I rang Umbro and asked them what the hell they were doing sending them to my house. They said sorry and that it was a mistake as they should have gone to the printers before being returned to them." The printing firm was based in Derbyshire. Rather than risk a problem – or so he thought – Chapple took it upon himself to drive the tops there himself. There the Kingstonian logo would be put on the tops before they were returned to Umbro for final inspection. Two days before the match the team went to their hotel, paid for by the FA. The tops still had not arrived. "I didn't panic," says Chapple. "Umbro knew I'd be away from the Thursday so I thought the tops would just turn up at Wembley and that they wouldn't let us down."

Forest Green Rovers had got their tops late and only by chance – they had arrived at The Lawn, their quaint stadium in the village of Nailsworth, Gloucestershire, twenty-four hours before the match. Luckily, there had been someone to take delivery of them and they were driven to north London. Not so Kingstonian's. They had been sent to Chapple's house after he had already left. "In the end we went out without them because we didn't have anything to wear," he says. "The Conference had a meeting about it and fined the club. It still makes me angry now. I'd driven all the way to Derby and then the Conference said that in their view we didn't want them because we had Grolsch on our shirts and they reckoned we wanted to flash that off. That was absolute rubbish. We could do that in the ninety minutes of the game. We didn't need to do that coming out on to the pitch."

As for the football, a tight game amid a wonderful atmosphere saw Tarkan Mustafa's goal separate the two sides on the hallowed turf. With two defences playing so superbly well, it was perhaps fitting that a right-back, not a forward, should conjure the winning goal. Mustafa's effort at the tunnel end of the ground was a thumping right-footer worthy of winning any match and proved that Kingstonian had players all over the pitch who could score goals.

Chapple had done it again. He took his time afterwards, did a press conference or two, and then quietly made his way to the bar. Privately he could have done without the celebrations, but he went through the formalities before finding time to reflect on another incredible day in his life.

For McNully it was a wonderful way to bow out as secretary as Derek Powell, a former Woking committee member who had joined Chapple at Kingsmeadow, took over. "I was around for the two Wembley triumphs although I retired as secretary after the first," says McNully. "I had a good relationship with Geoff and I always knew when something was going to happen because he'd say to me, 'stick around a bit later today Bill, we've got a bit of business to do.' That meant he was about to sign a player but he'd never let on who it was beforehand. I remember walking in to his office on one occasion and there was Leworthy sitting there. I couldn't believe my eyes and was always wondering who we were going to sign next. They were great times and those of us who were at the club at that time were spoilt by the quality of players he brought in. Geoff was slaughtered, quite wrongly, for spending money to get them in. Good players don't come cheap and in any case, the directors were the ones who were giving him permission to sign them. Without that he wouldn't have been able to do it."

Another good season in the Conference followed in 1999/00, with the seemingly inevitable Wembley trip to come in May – the last cup final to be played at the old stadium before the bulldozers moved in. Ks had hammered Sutton United in the semi-final, a far cry from the tension-filled Cheltenham ties that had taken place twelve months before.

The first leg was drawn at Sutton's Gander Green Lane. It was Chapple's first encounter with Sammy Winston, a player who would later join him at Kingstonian. "I remember reading the paper after they'd drawn the first game and Sammy had said the worst thing he could have – that they had seen nothing in our team to be frightened of in the second leg," he says. "He was full of it. Then we beat them 6-0." It was another game Chapple didn't see the end of as, once again, he was sat in the dressing room when the final whistle went. "I really had to sit and think about it," he says. "My mind was racing again. Was I human? Am I really alive? Even Chris Kelly said to me, 'I was God until you came here.' I was no such thing. I just had a good side. But getting to the final five times almost troubled me a bit and I thought, 'what is happening here?' What made it worse was that every time I went in to the dressing rooms at Wembley they had assistants who knew me so well their opening remark was, 'here he is again.'"

Kettering Town were Ks' opponents at Wembley and Chapple adds: "I was extra pleased with that because of Peter Mallinger their chairman. I always got on famously with him. I even got him a manager once – Gary Johnson. I told Peter I was chuffed for him that he was in the final."

Chapple's sense of humour came to the fore at that fifth Wembley final, with Powell – not only the secretary but a faithful friend – the butt of his practical joke. Despite Powell's loyalty, Chapple never missed a trick when it came to taking the rise out of him and Wembley 2000 was no exception. "Me and Derek have been good friends over the years," says Chapple. "He's a bit of a loner really. I've always been the same with him, playing tricks. He's lost his rag on more than one occasion. Anyway there was a Spanish barman named Monte at the Hogs Back Hotel. He was Deportivo La Coruña mad. He had an old green and gold waistcoat that he was going to throw away. If you actually put that waistcoat on it didn't look out of place with the players' suits they were wearing for the final. So we played a joke on Derek. We told the players that their suits would be ready at the hotel on a given night. Anyway, when we picked them up Derek's suit had a waistcoat with it, which he thought was part of the gear. Obviously he was the only one who had a waistcoat and on the day of the game he drove from our hotel while we went by coach. Everybody was in on the joke except poor Derek. We had to hide our laughs as we saw him wearing it while he was waiting in the Wembley tunnel. We got off the coach and his first remark to me was, 'Geoff, why am I the only one wearing a waistcoat?' I told him it was so bloody hot on the coach we'd taken them off. He kept his on all the way through the game, the reception afterwards and all evening."

Later that night, back at Kingstonian FC, Powell was listening to Chapple's speech when he suddenly realised he had been made a chump of. "I said: 'Ladies and gentleman before I say what I'm going to say, there's a certain person here this evening who I've badly stitched up and I want to apologise to,'" says Chapple. "Then as I looked up Derek was off out of the door. He knew what was coming." Powell remembers it well. "We've always played silly games together and it's generally all one way, directed at me," he says. "Some of the things he does, well, I'm surprised somebody hasn't landed him one. I've known him too long that's the trouble. If I'd known him only a week it would be different. He's done wind ups a few times but I've always let it ride."

Apart from the prank at Powell's expense, another notable thing about Chapple's final Wembley occasion happened off the pitch; alongside it in fact. Chapple's men trailed 2-1. It was the first time one of his teams had ever been behind at this stadium. A posse of cameramen gathered around the great man sitting on the Kingstonian bench. Like an eagle hovering over its prey, they smelt blood. Here was the big story – a Chapple defeat at Wembley. But they were to be disappointed and it was destined never to happen. However unlikely it seemed, Kingstonian struck twice in the final fifteen minutes to give Chapple a surely never to be beaten fifth triumph in seven years. But it had been oh so close. "I felt I was prepared to accept anything," he says. "It's a game played to the final whistle. We were behind and at that stage anything was possible. Of course within ten minutes we were back in front. At the final whistle I just got up and took the win in my stride. I was well aware that people were looking at me. I watched their faces around the Royal Box and they seemed genuinely pleased for me. Maybe they thought, 'he ain't such a bad guy and he's done it again. It must be his trophy.'"

Quite rightly the Football Association decided to award Chapple a replica of the FA Trophy. As a Chelsea fan nothing could beat being presented with his prize at Stamford Bridge and Steve Coppell was the man chosen to do the honours. It was all set up with the Umbro stage and hoardings in place, for the benefit of Sky TV. Then something funny happened. Chapple had always blamed Umbro for Kingstonian being fined after the 1999 final and he was never likely to forget it, even though they had more or less admitted their gaff by sending him a hold-all as a peace offering. "I went up on stage and there was Steve waiting to hand me the trophy," says Chapple. "There were cameras everywhere and as I walked across to him I tripped over the TV cables. As I fell, I had Steve in my arms and we went straight back through the Umbro boards. We're lying there prostrate and this guy named Duncan Thomson from Umbro came over and I said to him, 'that's for you and your previous cock up.' He knew what I meant."

Chapple was later voted non-League manager of the era, ahead of Barry Fry, Martin O'Neill and the like. It was another tremendous honour and Deadman is just one man who thinks Geoff thoroughly deserved the accolade. "As well as what he did at Woking, Geoff gave the fans at Kingstonian their happiest ever times," he says. "He was a supporters' man and how he used to deal with people, well I've never seen anybody like him. He had an open door policy for supporters and was always willing to talk. He wasn't one to show his emotions but I remember up at Southport for the FA Trophy quarter-final replay [14 March 2000]. We won 1-0 and at the end he was jumping for joy and came running across the pitch to share the moment with us fans. It was pelting down with rain and he had his cloth cap on which came off in the crowd. I'm not sure he ever got it back to be honest. It was an emotional time and I'd never seen him get like that. He was and still is a great man."

That 1999/00 season had been another season to match any other Chapple had completed in his twenty years as a football manager, but the following term would have bittersweet memories. The irony was that had it not been for a snap decision – formed at Wembley out of pure loyalty when his team had come from behind to beat Kettering – he may never have suffered relegation the following year and the sack for the first time in his life. Whereas he had decimated a Woking team earlier in his career by ruling with his head, this time his heart – bursting with pride in his men who had won him a fifth FA Trophy – was the dominant factor. Deep down he had known he had to change his team. But during that dramatic Wembley turnaround, the soft centre in Chapple emerged and he changed his mind. He would live to regret it.

9

Back to the Future

'They offered me a handshake of £10,000 to settle amicably. I told them they'd have to be a lot more amicable than that' – Tommy Docherty

Sometimes it happens out of the blue but more often than not, a football manager possesses a sixth sense when it comes to knowing he is about to be sacked. These days Geoff Chapple can't read a book without a pair of glasses perched on the end of his nose, but such is the efficiency of his long sight he could see the writing on any given wall from sixty paces. What he could not have foreseen though was being axed twice in seventeen months. After all here was a man who had held a job for thirteen years with Woking in his first spell; leaving of his own volition before enjoying a four-year stint at Kingstonian. Nevertheless, two sackings was to be his fate, and he had walked into his final meetings at both clubs with a clear vision of a P45 being waved in his face.

Losing his job at the end of his fourth season in charge of Kingstonian could not have been further from his mind at the start of the 2000/01 campaign though, with him having signed a new five-year contract. With hindsight he knows he should not have let his heart rule his head in the immediate aftermath of an FA Trophy win at Wembley the previous season when he knew he should change a Kingstonian side that was past its sell by date. He knew deep down he was making a mistake in keeping aging players such as Amara Simba – a French international – Mark Harris, Simon Stewart and Dave Leworthy, great servants though they had been. "Their legs were getting the better of them with due respect and I knew it was a time to change it," says Chapple. "Even before we had kicked a ball in the following season I knew that. But what happened [in the final] changed my mind. I remember sitting there in one or two of the game's dull moments planning ahead. And I decided to stick with it."

Front page of *The Non-League Paper* after Ks' win over Southend.

He had decided to stay loyal to his squad but he could not have imagined in his wildest dreams he would reach the fourth round of the FA Cup for the second time in his career, before suffering the agony of relegation and, ultimately, a trip to the local Job Centre. In fact Kingstonian were just seconds away from the fifth round, the last sixteen of the FA Cup, when they led Bristol City 1-0 at Ashton Gate. "Referee Graham Poll had added a minimum of three minutes and our centre half, Eddie

Saunders, went to head a ball clear but it flew off his head for a corner," Chapple recalls. "I remember looking up at the clock and when the corner was taken, three minutes and thirty-five seconds had gone. Then they scored from the corner. My blokes were lying on the floor crying their eyes out. We kicked off and Poll blew the whistle. It was that close. But I remember saying to the players, 'don't feel sorry, you have done fantastically well.' It doesn't matter whether a team scores in the first minute or the last, they all count. It was tough but I did say there might be a silver lining, as we might get the Sky TV replay which we did. We lost that second game 1-0 in the eighty-second minute. I didn't like myself that night because we weren't too adventurous and we tried to play it too tight. The more I think about it, Bristol City always had the edge and if anybody was going to nick it, it was them. So they were quite happy for us to keep it tight. We should have gone for it."

Chapple's love affair with the FA Cup had continued to flourish in that final year in top non-League management with Kingstonian. They had overcome a tough battle with Southport over two matches in the first round, before taking on and beating Brentford at Griffin Park in the second. Then, with the excitement and anticipation of the third round draw, came immediate disappointment when Chapple's men were paired with Southend United away at Roots Hall. It represented a no-win situation, with most pundits expecting them to lose while there was little glory in winning. "Eddie Akuamoah scored early for us and then we had a player sent off," says Chapple. "When the players came in at half-time I pulled off striker Sammy Winston and put on David Bass, a midfield player. The others looked at me as if to say, 'what are you doing?'"

Chapple had worked out Southend's one and only game plan, that of slinging the ball out to the wings and getting the ball into the box as soon as possible. "They did it perfectly," he says. "They did it every five minutes. So I sent my team out in the second half to defend our lead as best we could. Southend couldn't break us down and we won 1-0."

But the Kingstonian directors were hardly supportive of their manager, even in this moment of glory. It was to be the case for the remainder of the season. "Chris Kelly came up to me afterwards and all he said was it was the worst game of football he'd ever seen in his life," says Chapple. "It was an absolute disgrace for him to say that. We'd just got in to the fourth round of the FA Cup. That wasn't bad was it?"

Star midfielder Geoff Pitcher backs up Chapple's story. "Kelly said that to me too," he reveals. "He said something like, 'that wasn't a good game was it?' My reply was, 'I don't care; we're in the last thirty-two of the FA Cup.' That was typical of him. He was a strange one to deal with. In the end there were all sorts of things going on at that club."

Kelly had his reasons and says: "Geoff got himself up for the cup games and seemed to get an adrenalin rush from them but our FA Cup run was just masking the problems in the League. I knew back in the September, after we'd played five games, that we needed to bring in new players. I told Geoff then that unless he did something about it we'd be relegated. He refused to do anything and that was an insult to everyone who had put money in and worked so hard. Basically he got lazy in that last season. He didn't go to games, or sign anybody. In fact in the end he wasn't doing anything. I would have backed him if he'd wanted to sign players but he did nothing when relegation was avoidable. That's why I wasn't happy in the cup games and why I wasn't upset that we didn't beat Bristol City in the fourth round because I knew we'd be on Sky for the replay and we could get some money back from that."

Kingstonian's results were not great leading up to the cup run and they suffered even more after it as the club began to spiral towards the relegation places. "What I said about needing new players was not a personal affront to Geoff, although he thought it was," adds Kelly. "It was for the good of the club. He thought he could get by on his reputation and in the end there were players coming to me and telling me something had to be done. They hadn't lost respect for Geoff as a person, just for what was going on at that moment in time."

While people maintain that Kelly was jealous of Chapple's success, he categorically denies it. "I'd had my fifteen minutes of fame twenty-five years beforehand," he says. "Geoff was on a substantial salary, twice as much as me and I was full-time. But I didn't begrudge him that because in the first three seasons what he did for the club was phenomenal and no-one can take his record away. He was 'the boss' and he was a brilliant manager for three years. But in the end he wasn't earning his money and didn't behave in a way I would have expected from someone with his reputation. I still have the utmost respect for his managerial record, even though he didn't come cheap and there was a price to pay for the success he had."

For Chapple – who maintains he was on £32,500 at the time as compared to Kelly's reported £20,000, and therefore not double – the season was becoming a chore, not least because of activities off the pitch. "It was starting to become a horrible season all round," he says. "The directors didn't want to come to games. I remember up at Northwich when Derek Powell [secretary] was trying to do everything. He was here, there and in the boardroom. I told my assistant Ian McDonald to take the team while I went into the boardroom so that Derek could do his secretarial duties. It was a horrible time and I felt totally isolated. I was close to the supporters though and I think that got up the directors' noses. The fans backed me to the hilt with everything."

Before Chapple was removed from his job, McDonald was ousted and such is the way of things in football, the former Aldershot midfielder was unhappy that Chapple didn't follow suit. "I was disappointed with Geoff because I felt we were both to blame but I got all of it," says McDonald. "I do understand the reasons Geoff stayed but a lot of the anger in me came from the fact that I tried to talk to him about what was needed and he wouldn't listen. Players like Gary Patterson and Phil Wingfield needed operations in the May at the end of the previous season but didn't get them until August and missed the first fifteen games of the new season. In fact there were four players out at the start of the season and Geoff's answer was to fill the gaps with loan players. I thought we should replace them and knew we were in trouble in September. But Geoff wouldn't do it and told me that he would only start to panic if we were in the same situation in January. If it wasn't for the FA Cup run I think he'd have listened sooner but in the end it was too late. I think Geoff's a bit of a loner really and he wanted to do things his way. But I don't think that's right when you're in a partnership."

Despite his resentment at Chapple not sticking by him in his hour of need – in his eyes at least – McDonald admits he is gobsmacked that no-one has approached his former boss. "Perhaps people think he'll need a budget to be successful but it's very surprising," he adds. "I really enjoyed my time with Geoff and I owe a lot to him because he took me on when I lost my job at Portsmouth. He let me get on with the coaching and gave me the players on a plate. He is a great man, had great enthusiasm for the game and was a great talker. He had that aura about him which helped him get the best out of his players. He had a good eye for a player too. Although we didn't always see eye to eye on that, seven out of ten times he'd be right. I just felt in the end he could have been more loyal to me."

Chapple does not have fond memories of that time. "It caused a lot of upset when the club got rid of Ian and I stayed," he says. "It was a horrible situation. Ian was made a scapegoat. But I had no choice. In an ideal world I should have gone but I was struggling financially with a house to keep and a broken marriage. The departing person always feels bitter and Macca was bitter. It took a while for us to get ourselves together again."

Murmurings from directors about how fit the players looked had been going on for some time at training nights. Now the directors had acted. "I think they had wanted Ian out for a long time but I fought tooth and nail to keep him," insists Chapple. "At the time he went the club were hoping we would both go anyway. After all it wasn't Ian's fault we were struggling. But it angered me that he was being questioned. He was a real 100 per center and did a fantastic job."

Colin Deadman, Kingstonian FC's supporters' club chairman, thinks Chapple and McDonald were treated appallingly in those final months at Kingstonian. "The directors manipulated it so that it caused problems for Ian and Geoff, which made me angry," he says. "They thought Geoff would walk with Ian when Ian was sacked, but when he didn't they made it a situation where Geoff came out looking the bad guy. The problem was that the club's profile had been raised so high that the admin side and the financial side couldn't keep up. The directors were not able to cope with the success."

McDonald still can't understand why he was dumped and adds: "I thought it was a very hasty decision from the directors at the time and they didn't seem to care two hoots for my previous record. They were not supportive to either Geoff or myself. We had finished respectably for two seasons, won the Trophy twice and had a great FA Cup run. But that wasn't enough for them."

While McDonald was the first to go, the end of the season would bring to an end Chapple's era too. Relegation had become a reality at Chester in a 0-0 draw as the season drew to a close, but the nature of his sacking was a strange scenario. "It was a weird ending to my life at Kingstonian," he says. "I was addressing the supporters in the club bar one night. They had been fantastic to me. I told them we'd had a bad year despite a great cup run and that we should stick together, regroup and hope to be back in the Conference the following season."

The fans, including Deadman, hung on his every word but little did Chapple know, the decision to get rid of him had already been made.

"The board had already met and I'd been sacked," he says. Having the bottle to tell him he had lost his job seemed to be proving difficult for chairman Alan Kingston though and Chapple recalls: "He was virtually hanging on to my shirt tails that night. He was so close, he didn't leave me alone. At the end of the night he came out of the door with me and walked me to the car. I think he wanted to tell me then but he just couldn't. Instead, he rang me the next day saying we needed a meeting to decide which League we wanted to go in, the Ryman or Southern Premier. He told me to make some inquiries and we'd meet that night to discuss it."

Chapple wasn't about to fall for the devious ploy. "I'm not daft," he says. "I knew what was happening and that if he turned up on his own he might have been telling me the truth. If he turned up with a legal representative, then I'd be gone." The inevitable happened. "He turned up with a solicitor," he adds. "So I asked him what it was he needed to tell me and he said the board had requested a change. I said: 'Right, I signed a five-year contract a year ago so pay it up and we're okay.'" Chapple was flabbergasted by the response which was that 'it was a bit difficult' and the club were only prepared to give him £5,000. "I got up and said, 'thanks for the meeting, see you in court then,'" says Chapple. On his way out of the room, he could hear the aptly named Kingston calling him back, telling him to wait. "I was going," he says. "But in the end I went back and settled for an ex-gratia payment which was virtually nothing compared to what they owed me. They got away lightly and I didn't pursue it because it would have taken years to come to court. I had to live and I needed money. In the end they brought in Bill Williams as manager and upped the budget, which seemed a bit odd."

Deadman confirms: "You could tell how underhand the directors were because after Geoff had gone the club advertised the manager's job in *The Non League Paper* on Sunday," he says. "On the Monday, the very next day, at around 4p.m., Bill Williams was appointed, so they'd obviously already done it."

For his time at Kingstonian to end in such a way was sad for a man who had taken the club into the Conference for the first time and won two FA Trophy finals at Wembley. Short-sightedness is a common trait in football these days and while the Ks' directors had their reasons for making their decision, it is pertinent to mention that the club has never been the same since and has lurched from one financial crisis to another.

The irony of McDonald later returning to manage Kingstonian in the Ryman League is not lost on Chapple and having got back on good terms with his former assistant, he would like nothing better than for him to be successful in management.

Former secretary Bill McNully also believes Chapple was dealt with shabbily by the directors. "To be honest the way he was treated at the end was diabolical," he says. "It was stupid to get rid of him. We'd already been relegated and Geoff had seven or eight names he was going to bring in. But he was worshipped by the fans and the directors didn't like that. Chris Kelly for instance didn't like the fact that Geoff became more popular than him. I think it was a racing certainty that Kelly was jealous of him and there was no doubt Geoff had got bigger than the club. But he'd be welcomed back tomorrow by the supporters."

The man who took over from McNully as secretary, Powell, adds: "When I took the job on I told Geoff I would only deal with him, not the directors. I made a statement to that effect. Chris Kelly was chief executive but I never dealt with him. I just did what I had to on the football side – that was the most important thing. We had great times in the FA Trophy and FA Cup and made a few pennies, although where the money went I don't know. They [the directors] were funny people. They'd say one thing to your face and then stab you in the back. I think the reason they got rid of Geoff was down to money. They couldn't afford him. They wanted to cut the wage bill and the quickest way to do that was to get rid of the manager. I knew what was happening and that I'd be going as well."

Terry Weir, the man who had brought Chapple to Kingstonian, was gone from the scene by then, disillusioned by what he called "too many people with too big egos" at the club. "I found that difficult, but Geoff's time at Kingstonian had been the greatest time ever," he says.

The next chapter in Chapple's life was about to follow. It would involve making a dramatic return to Kingfield as manager of his beloved Woking. He had actually helped install Colin Lippiatt as Cards' boss in March 2000, the plan being for Chapple to take over not long after and for Lippiatt to go back to being his assistant. But Lippiatt almost single-handedly saved Woking from relegation that year, having taken over from Brian McDermott. Chapple's faithful number two had enjoyed his time in charge of the Cards. So much so, he was quite happy to continue the job on his own. After all, he had already picked up invaluable experience at Yeovil Town and felt more comfortable being in the front line.

So Chapple didn't return to Kingfield in the summer of 2000 and instead he signed his new five-year deal a few miles down the road in Kingston. But it wasn't long before Chapple, out of work and available following his sacking a year later, got a call from Lippiatt and ended up breezing through the gates of Kingfield once again to take over. "I'd gone to see Woking *v.* Newport County in the FA Cup fourth qualifying round, just minding my own business," he says. "I paid to go in on my own but still got zapped by a photographer. Warren Patmore missed a great chance with a header in the last minute. If that had gone in and Woking had won, I don't think anything would have happened. But Woking lost 3-1 in the replay and Colin rang me after that game in a terrible state. He wanted me to come back. So to be fair to Colin he got me back to the club, although reading between the lines he might well have been going himself if he hadn't. I wasn't doing anything then but the club had to get rid of Kevan Brown to get me in, which was sad for Kevan. I went back on a pittance but after I'd signed, Colin said he felt like a new man. I think the weight had been lifted off his shoulders."

Chapple knew immediately how difficult his task was going to be but maintains: "I was happy to go back because it felt right. I have no regrets. I liked the people there but it was very different to how I wanted it to be when I went back. It was harder and I never had my own players. I told Colin I'd have to meet the players on the Thursday, two days before my first game against Hereford. So we got them all in and we went in the dressing room to see them. Well, I couldn't believe what I was seeing. They were sitting on the benches, standing on the benches. There were more than twenty players in there. And they were all for one team as there was no reserves at the time. I thought to myself, 'no wonder I've got a job.' Half of them hadn't played for weeks and someone said to me they didn't want to either. They were still getting their money and that's all that mattered to some of them."

Chapple's vision for the future was clear. The old adage 'never go back' may have crossed his mind but he quickly cast aside any doubts about his ability to improve the Cards' flagging fortunes. But the honeymoon period did not last too long as Lippiatt, who had soon realised that it wouldn't work out with his friend, became history himself. At a board meeting, with talk of his position nowhere near any agenda for the evening, it was mooted that perhaps the assistant manager was surplus to requirements and should be sacked. It did not take long for the deed to be done.

But having achieved a Houdini act to save Woking the previous season, Lippiatt was understandably bitter and fell out with Chapple over the matter, a dispute which has left a wound that is yet to heal fully. Lippiatt believes that Chapple knew what was happening and should have stood up for him, or left himself. Chapple sees it differently and vehemently denies there was a campaign to ditch his friend. "I knew absolutely nothing about it and to me it felt like a bereavement," he maintains. So Chapple stayed put and quickly brought in former Southampton midfielder Glenn Cockerill as his assistant, a recommendation from Dennis Rofe at the South Coast club.

The emergence of a new chairman and owner of Woking FC, multimillionaire Chris Ingram, saved Woking from oblivion after the club hit severe financial trouble, with an annual loss soon to hit £500,000. The money worries meant it would prove difficult to build a team. "I remember Chris ringing me up saying, 'you do understand that a £7,500 budget is a £7,500 budget?'" says Chapple, who knew the score.

The Cards finished fourth from bottom of the Conference in 2001/02 under Chapple. However, the following season began with a bang as he lifted Woking to top of the Conference by the end of August. But a series of drubbings the following month – including a humiliating 5-1 home reverse against bitter rivals Stevenage Borough – finally took their toll. "It was at a time when I was still trying to reduce a heavy budget down to something that was acceptable to the club," Chapple reflects. "So basically any player who came to the end of his contract was finished at Woking and I couldn't replace them. One of the straws that broke the camel's back concerned Roscoe D'Sane, who I had on non-contract and who I thought was going to be a great prospect for us. He wanted me to double his wages from £250 a week to £500 or more and I couldn't. Aldershot could. So I advised him to take their offer. All the time this was happening I was getting beatings and I'm not used to beatings."

It was a period, in a traumatic and dramatic 2002/03 season, which would be remembered by Woking supporters as 'Black September' – and Chapple was the man under fire. "I was getting abuse from the fans which I'd never had before," he recalls. "It was only a minority but they made enough noise. It was hard and it was painful. I had some nice letters of support but after one game another said, 'I don't know you Mr Chapple. But after sitting through that debacle would you please send me my admittance money back in the post.' I saw her husband soon after that and he said: 'I admire you Geoff because you actually replied to her letter without being nasty.' I said: 'I always do.'"

Chapple remembers a board meeting where a plan was formed for taking Woking Football Club into the full-time era. "They [the directors] agreed to put up a little bit more money because we were struggling big time to attract players," he says. "We had the likes of Robert Kember, who would bust a leg for us, but on real low money. The players I brought in the second time around were hard workers but they weren't Woking type players. We were scrabbling around trying to find £150 and £200 a week for anybody we could get. I had Dean Hooper, a good old friend of mine who wanted to come and play for me. I told him I couldn't do it, so he went to Aldershot too. Aldershot were recruiting and we were getting rid. I'm not criticising because the budget had to be brought down from a high level. Anyway, the directors agreed to give us more money, but in the end I didn't have enough time to use it."

His last ever game in charge of the Cards came at Haig Avenue, Southport, just as it had for Brian McDermott back in February 2000. "I was sitting opposite Glenn [Cockerill] on the way to that Southport game and we were ringing up people like Paul Gascoigne, just to see if they could turn out for us because we were so short of players," says Chapple. "Glenn had to play himself, which was an embarrassment. We were winning 1-0 for an hour and we lost 5-1 after Glenn, who was playing well, brought himself off. I was absolutely shell-shocked because it had been another beating and we had been losing by four and five goals. I remember our goalkeeper Shwan Jalal was standing there afterwards stunned and he just said, 'sorry, I did what I could mate.' I told him I wasn't blaming him. Obviously various people noticed my body language on the coach coming home from that game, including Phil Ledger [football director] and Brian Blower [managing director], because I felt it badly. I don't know for sure but I'm pretty confident in my own mind that talks about getting rid of me happened that night among the directors."

Chapple knew the writing was on the wall when chairman and club owner Ingram summoned him to a 9a.m. meeting on the Monday at Kingfield, two days after his miserable journey home. His mind was still in disarray. "I saw the chairman as arranged and Glenn [Cockerill] was due in after me at 10.15a.m.," he says. "I spoke to Glenn beforehand. I don't know whether he knew anything because I certainly didn't."

Somebody knew something though and it didn't take a genius for Chapple to work out who. "The sad thing was that when I went in to Kingfield to meet Chris [Ingram], it was like a ghost town," Chapple recalls. "It was as if it had all been primed. There was no-one about. But as I walked out afterwards, Brian Blower said, 'best of luck mate.' So he already knew didn't he?"

As for that final discussion with his chairman, Chapple adds: "The meeting was amicable. I made Chris a cup of tea and we sat down and had a chat, albeit a brief one. We talked about things not going as well as we'd liked and that it would be best to draw a line under it. I knew it was coming, I'm not daft. I knew from the Sunday night when I had rung Phil Ledger and told him Glenn and I were seeing Chris the next day. I asked Phil what it was all about and he said, 'I've told him [Ingram] not to panic because I've seen it all before'. What he probably said to Chris was, 'don't panic, don't get rid of both of them.'"

Chapple kept his promise to speak to Cockerill after his chat with the chairman and adds: "I rang him and said, 'best of luck, it's yours mate.' He came out with the usual, 'do you want me to resign?' But those things aren't going to happen. Then sod's law, they go and beat Chester 1-0 on the Saturday after I'm gone."

Cockerill maintains he knew as much as Chapple about what was happening. "Geoff came out of his meeting and told me he'd been sacked and that was the first I knew," he says. "I said, 'well that's the end of me then' but Geoff said, 'not necessarily, I think they want to give you a go.' I told him I'd walk too but he said to me, 'no, you stay and give it a go.'"

Cockerill did stay and, following a trial period, went on to take the job permanently. But he knows he owes Chapple a debt of gratitude for giving him a job at Kingfield and has kept in touch, while, having led Woking to the 2006 FA Trophy final against Grays Athletic, he was hoping to involve his old boss in some way. "We never fell out, it was one of those things," adds Cockerill. "I enjoyed working with him as he was jovial and full of life. He was a great character who got players in who wanted to play for him. He had something about him. What happened was unfortunate and I think in the end there were players who really let him down. There should have been a role for him at Woking though, maybe on the commercial side. Now he's enjoying life at Farnham and I think he's quite happy there. It's his choice he's not doing something else."

Ledger adds: "I'll always regard Geoff as a friend but when he came back it was different and things had moved on in the game. It had changed at such a rate and it was difficult for him to get it back to how it was. It was sad how it ended for him. But he was unique. I would put my life on the fact that nobody will ever match his record of five Wembley wins in seven years."

Chapple has no axe to grind with Ingram or Ledger, the former having told the media it had been a resignation in an effort to make the whole situation more honourable. In the event not many in the local press were naïve enough to buy that line. After all if somebody wanted to resign, why would they choose to fight their way through the rush hour traffic to do it? "To be honest Chris looked after me," says Chapple of Ingram. "I'm a very good reader of characters. You've got to be to be a football manager. Chris was fine; it was a very amicable parting. He did make sure that if I wasn't going to work for six months or so, he'd look after me. He was probably sad about having to sack me because he was brought up on football when I was there before."

After Chapple had left the club, Woking continued to have a roller-coaster season, with a series of strange result sequences, until their survival boiled down to the last game at home to Telford United. By the skin of their teeth, and thanks to rivals, Farnborough Town and Stevenage Borough, both winning on the final day, Woking avoided relegation and survived to fight another day in the Conference. Chapple was happy about that. "I'd been out of it since October so I'd been gone about seven months by then," he says. "I was at home that day keeping an eye on the results. I was genuinely pleased they stayed up."

Nobody would have expected him to feel any different about Woking's survival and you only have to look into his eyes when he says it to know he means every word.

10

Brothers in Arms

'A true friend is one who stabs you in the front' – Oscar Wilde

"Like Clough and Taylor we were," says Geoff Chapple. And there is no doubting the twinkle in his eye as he recalls life with Colin Lippiatt, the man who became his best friend and close ally. "We'd be on the phone together like a couple of old women three times a day," he adds. "He was like a brother to me. Hand on heart, I can honestly say we wouldn't have achieved half the things we did at Woking if it hadn't been for Colin. He never really got the recognition he deserved but he played a big part in our success."

It is a glowing endorsement and one that matches the illumination on Chapple's face as he recalls the times he shared with Lippiatt at Woking and Kingstonian. There is genuine warmth exuding from his features at mention of the name Lippiatt, who was sixty-five on 1 January 2006. Theirs is a relationship which, for better or worse, has lasted a good twenty-five years.

While the two men have rarely spoken since Lippiatt's departure from Woking Football Club in late 2001 – at which time the pair had an acrimonious fall out – it doesn't alter the fact they were made for each other. "We got on from virtually day one, there were no issues at all," says Lippiatt, who hopes to continue his time as boss of Nationwide Conference club St Albans into 2007 and possibly beyond. "Early on I had a lot of energy and desire, although I would never have called myself ambitious. Geoff's style was that he left me alone to do the coaching, the training and the preparation. I just got on with what I wanted to do. I enjoyed it and over the years, without wanting to sound arrogant, I grew into the job more and more as I gained experience. We had a great relationship and we had some good times. We mustn't forget that we had a very good social time together as well. We went out quite a lot and when I had my sixtieth birthday Geoff was one of the guests. You don't invite people along like that unless you have an affinity and a bond with that person."

However, there are now problems between the pair and Lippiatt admits to feeling distant from the man with whom he spent so much time during his life in senior football. "Being honest, in the present, I don't feel quite that closeness there once was," he adds. "It's not to do with still being bitter, because I'm not. What happens is your own life goes on and there are different issues in life to deal with. Now I'm doing a manager's job again and I never thought I'd be doing that. I know results make a big difference in football, but I now feel more at home than I've ever felt in terms of feeling comfortable with doing what I'm doing. I did say I'd never be a manager again but I'm happy because of the environment I'm in. Again, it's not arrogance but I don't need the job and I don't need the money so there's no pressure on me."

Together Chapple and Lippiatt achieved more than they could possibly have imagined as a management duo. And physio Barry Kimber, a wonderful servant to Woking Football Club spanning three decades, can count himself part of Chapple's special harem.

The Chapple/Lippiatt managerial double act began in the 1986/87 season at Woking but they were more than just acquaintances long before then. They had met on that far off night when a young Chapple scored the equaliser for Alton Town against Windsor & Eton in the Athenian League Cup final. Then joint Windsor manager, Lippiatt had approached the influential Alton midfielder after that game and asked him to come and play for The Royalists. It didn't happen straight away but the wheels were in motion and it wasn't long before Chapple, along with three of his Alton teammates, Chris Yates, Bobby King and Ross McCulloch, decided to take Lippiatt up on his offer to help make Windsor the kings of the castle.

But the real bonding between the two larger-than-life characters began when they linked up at Kingfield as manager and assistant before embarking on a crusade through the lower levels of the non-League pyramid. Right from the word go, they were compatible. "The good thing about Colin was that if he liked a player you could bet your life that I would too," says Chapple. "We seemed to have this thing going, which I don't think we realised at the time, about special players. That's just the way it was."

Lippiatt acknowledges the fact and adds: "I always believed one of my strengths was that I could get the best out of players or improve them, even if it was only a small percentage. Geoff and I both wanted to play the passing game and we had the same philosophy. That will never change."

Chapple can't recall exactly why it was the pair joined forces but thinks it may have developed from the amount of time they used to spend on the phone together. "My previous assistant, Phil Darren, left Woking in the summer of 1986 and obviously I couldn't do it on my own, so in came Colin," he says. "In those early years Colin and I had the likes of Paul Shrubb, Fred Callaghan, Ernie Howe and Derek Cotterill all come in to help us at any one time. Things didn't always go to plan with three of us. It used to ruffle a few feathers."

So why three on the management team? "Colin and I always felt we could do with another coach, even though we probably could have got by without," he adds. "In the end they all came and went. Of course coaches have all got minds of their own. They probably suggested things to me but Colin would say, 'look I'm the assistant manager' and we'd end up doing it his way. He probably felt a bit insecure but he had no reason to feel like that."

Not many people in non-League football can come anywhere close to Lippiatt's encyclopedic knowledge of players, while Chapple rated him as a coach. "He was no mug and knew what he wanted," he says. "And that was to play the ball on the floor. He was a great one for that. By and large it was a great partnership, fantastic, better than I could have ever hoped for. I thought he was a very important cog in what I was trying to do. He was second to none at getting in players. I would pick up the phone and say to Colin, 'we could do with so and so' and the deal would be done in five minutes. He doesn't mess around. He got Clive Walker and Laurence Batty in. That's the sort of thing he was doing. There aren't many people in the game with a map of the non-League like Colin. It's far more expansive than mine, even though I remember an insurance colleague of mine once saying that my black book would be worth a million quid to him."

At a time when Chapple was working ridiculous hours at the Prudential Assurance Company, while also trying to be a football manager, Lippiatt was invaluable. He shouldered a lot of the burden and in Chapple's words, "was the perfect foil who made my job a lot easier."

Once into his stride on the subject of his old sidekick, it is not difficult to see the affection Chapple still has for Lippiatt, his eyes dancing around happily as the memories of their time together come flooding back. "He was infectious," he adds. "The two of us had a bloody exciting partnership, because of the things that were happening. He was generous and we both did things for the team out of our own pockets. He used to make me laugh too because he threw his wobblys. I went to a wedding once and left him in charge when we played Brentford in a friendly. He rang me at the wedding and told me he'd let me down badly. I said, 'what's up?' and he said, 'I've had a fight with Bradley Pratt [Woking centre half].' That got to boardroom level to sort out. Even though Colin is a very sociable character and likes a laugh, he can lose it sometimes and get angry."

For his part, Lippiatt can recall the odd hilarious moment himself and says: "We went across to Dorking once for a Surrey Senior Cup tie. We had a particular player in our dressing room before the game and Geoff called me outside and said, 'you got a minute?' Then he said to me, 'what's that bloke doing in our dressing room? You better go in there and tell him this is the away dressing room, he should be in the home one.' When I asked him who he meant he went back in and said, 'that lad over there in the corner.' I said to Geoff, 'that's Lee Davidson, who plays in our reserves.' Geoff thought he was a Dorking player and didn't know he was playing for us that night."

Chapple recalls one of the many trips they went on together – the time they ventured north to watch Billingham Synthonia before an FA Trophy tie early in 1994. "We went up with Len Holland, one of the committee members," says Chapple. "It was pretty wintry and we got outside the ground at quarter to seven and there was nobody there, it was dead. We were a bit annoyed as we'd driven five hours to get there. We thought the game was off so we drove around a bit but thought we better take another look. So not long after 7p.m. we went back and parked up outside the ground. We were soon aware of these lights behind us and then cars started to turn up one by one. We soon discovered that, apparently, the players changed somewhere else and then came to the ground. So we decided we'd go in one at a time unannounced and change our accents. We all had flat caps on. I just didn't want them to know we were there."

Chapple and his two companions did not expect there to be a crowd of less than fifty though, which jeopardised somewhat their attempts to look inconspicuous and to blend in. "One side of the ground was completely open with a railing fence and I was the only one standing there," Chapple laughs. "Len was huddled up at the back of the big stand opposite and Colin was in the middle of us. Looking back it was crazy but we used to leave no stone unturned. By seeing other teams Colin and I would get a feel for how we would do. It was weird and hard to describe but I always knew if I saw a side, I would start to get a bit excited thinking we'd got a chance of beating them. We drove away from Billingham's ground in an absolute blizzard with me driving, poor old Colin navigating and Len curled up on the back seat asleep under my blanket. We got home about 3a.m."

Another time that made Chapple laugh was before the FA Cup fourth round clash with Everton in 1991. "We flew up to watch them and before the flight at Gatwick, Colin saw Su Pollard, who used to be in *Hi De Hi*," he says. "He didn't know her personally. Anyway we were together and suddenly Colin had disappeared. I turned around and there he was with Su, all over her giving her hugs and kisses as though they were long-lost friends. He was a great character and that's just the way he was."

Chapple always viewed Lippiatt as more than just an ally and adds: "In our period of time together we were very close. It's almost as if we were family. We did a lot together, went to see lots of games together and I enjoyed his company immensely. We had some great laughs and he was very passionate about Woking, which was vitally important at the time because we were going though a period where we were getting bigger and bigger as a club."

Lippiatt left Chapple a couple of times in the early years but like true marriages with substance, both men kissed and made up and hardly a day passed when they weren't on the phone to each other. "Colin was always telling me he didn't want to be a manager," says Chapple. "As my assistant at Woking he once wrote to me saying he was going to pursue a career somewhere else. But wherever he said he was going, he never went. Then he came back."

The pair got into some scrapes together and Chapple remembers the time when one of his players tried to attack him – thanks to a comment made by Lippiatt. "We were up at Halifax and Junior Hunter [striker] took exception to a remark that had been made on the way back into the dressing room after the game," says Chapple. "Junior had been sent off and some words were said to him that were unrepeatable. Junior thought it was me who said it but it wasn't. Colin had said something as we were all walking in and Junior had to be restrained from getting in the dressing room because he was after me at the time. If he'd got in he'd have killed me. He was screaming out loud and he was so strong. Someone had to take him home in a private car because he couldn't come home with us that night. It all got patched up afterwards and looking back it was funny, although it was quite nasty at the time."

Lippiatt admits: "It was me who said it. Junior was ranting and raving and then I shouted at him to shut up. It was just a personal comment in a strong, positive way. But Junior lost the plot and thought that Geoff had said it. He had to go home in Jon Taylor's car [director] in the end."

An indication of Chapple's loyalty towards his side-kick came in 1994 when Cards' chairman Ted Hills gave him permission to speak to Aldershot Town, a club he had always supported, although it was more an affair of the heart than deep-rooted love. When The Shots came calling, Chapple went for an interview with Hills' counterpart Terry Owens and his decision to turn down the position was in no small part down to Owens' reluctance to take Lippiatt too. Lippiatt admits he was never made aware of that fact. "Aldershot passed me by because I turned them down," confirms Chapple. "I was surprised that Ted [Hills] gave them permission to talk to me in the first place. But he did, so I met Terry Owens and Colin met him separately. I went back again for another meeting with Terry and in the end he said, 'you've got the job.' I said, 'thank you very much,' although I didn't accept it at that time. Then he said, 'but we won't be taking Mr Lippiatt.' So that had a bearing on my thoughts. I told him I'd meet him at the Hogs Back Hotel in Farnham on a given day and I would give him my decision."

Chapple already knew in his heart what he intended to do as he walked in through the hotel doors for a final rendezvous with the Shots' chairman. "I sat down with him to talk and I can still see him now putting half a sausage in his mouth when I said, 'by the way I'm staying at Woking.' They weren't going to take Colin and I wasn't happy about that, because we went as a pair. So I stuck by Colin then. There were also other things happening at Woking I was excited about, such as the new stand which was about to be built, and I had great support from Woking council at that time. So I stayed at Kingfield and have never regretted that decision."

In the summer of 1997, against the background of player unrest and discontent off the pitch, Chapple and Lippiatt did both leave Kingfield.

Only this time together, to Kingstonian. Lippiatt recalls that fateful meeting at former Woking chairman Jon Davies' house prior to the duo leaving for pastures new. And he is adamant that Davies was well wide of the mark in assuming he and Chapple had lined up a move elsewhere. "As far as I'm concerned that was absolute rubbish," he says. "We had no intention of going anywhere. I'm not just saying that because I was there but as soon as we walked in it was pretty obvious there seemed to be an issue on Jon's mind. When he asked, 'where are you going?' it wasn't the best start to a meeting and subconsciously you're bound to wonder whether he wanted us to go. Maybe he had someone else in mind and that's the only reason I can come up with as to why he came out and said what he did."

John McGovern's appointment as Woking manager, after he and Chapple left, surprised and disappointed Lippiatt, who adds: "My view is a little contentious. I think the non-League game has been what I call infested with Football League people. Quite frankly I think there are people in the game disillusioned by that. I also think some are being led up the garden path thinking it's the right way to go. There are many good non-League people out there who are quite capable of taking a team out of the Conference into the Football League."

Chapple and Lippiatt always seemed to end up back together after the few times they parted. One of those occasions was when Chapple created an opening at Kingstonian for his old mate when Lippiatt left the manager's job at Yeovil Town. The Somerset club wanted someone to go full-time and Lippiatt wasn't interested. Returning the favour, Lippiatt took Chapple back to Woking the second time around in late 2001, although Chapple was supposed to have gone back to Kingfield a lot sooner than that.

Chapple explains: "At the end of 2000, when I was at Kingstonian, I got a phone call out of the blue from someone high up at Woking asking whether I'd be prepared to go back there," says Chapple. "I couldn't at the time because I was under contract at Kingstonian until the summer and this was in February. So I got Colin back in there as Woking's manager instead. I got my representatives together and we had various meetings with Woking directors, the plan being for Colin to go in as manager, then I would join him as and when. Everything was thrashed out and I remember my representative standing up and saying: 'right gentlemen, do we all understand the scenario? Mr Lippiatt will be installed as your manager in the interim until Mr Chapple is free to come back. Mr Lippiatt will then revert to first team coach.' It was all sorted out."

However, the plan never came to fruition as Lippiatt – who had saved the club from relegation since returning on his own – decided, so Chapple thought, he didn't want anyone else's help, and that included his former boss. Lippiatt, the man who always maintained he did not want to be a number one, was enjoying being just that. "When the time came for us to have a final meeting it never happened," says Chapple. "The directors at Woking told me Colin had thrown his toys out of the pram about me coming back so that was that. Colin knew the agreement but it was never allowed to get off the ground so I just let it happen. I stayed at Kingstonian instead and gladly signed a new five-year deal, which I only got to see a year of."

Lippiatt saw the situation differently and insists: "I would have had no problems with Geoff coming back. Yes, I was quite happy to carry on on my own. But there were other issues concerning whether the club could afford to have Geoff back because he was on a contract at Kingstonian. It wasn't just down to me. And I wasn't going to leave just because Geoff wasn't coming back. When I had gone there Woking were as good as down, it was that serious. We ended up in a decent position in the end so I feel as though I achieved something good by keeping them up."

Chapple's extended spell at Kingstonian was cut short by his sacking in the summer of 2001 and so it was that Lippiatt eventually needed his friend's help and they paired up again at Woking not long into the 2001/02 season. Their reunion depended on Lippiatt making a decision which he deeply regrets. He had to get rid of his number two, former Kingfield favourite Kevan Brown, who was known as 'Captain Marvel' in his first playing spell at Woking. Brown was sacrificed so his wages could be added to the pot to bring Chapple back in. "I lost a very good friendship with Kevan, one which I'd had for many years," says Lippiatt. "That was a big blow to me personally and I dropped a clanger there. It's no good denying it. It was upsetting, although as time goes by it erodes a little bit. When I think about it, I know I let Kevan down big time."

Lippiatt's subsequent dismissal, just a short while into his and Chapple's renewed partnership, was the catalyst for acrimony. And the bitterness felt by Lippiatt over his departure still lingers to a degree. "I was glad to be out of the spotlight when Geoff came in and the board backed my proposal to bring him back, saying it was my decision," he says. "Then

Geoff and I had a disagreement over something petty during a cup game and I realised it was a mistake. We were by the dugout and while the disagreement wasn't anything heavy, I remember turning to him and saying 'this isn't going to work out'. It was only over a substitution or something like that and it was only about our third game together. The trouble is I'd become a manager and although I'd stepped aside, I didn't find it easy."

Lippiatt's sacking came as a hammer blow one Tuesday morning, the day after a board meeting. "The phone call came from John Buchanan [vice chairman] and whatever you say about getting the sack, it's not very nice," says Lippiatt. "Especially over the phone – although I'd done that to Kevan [Brown] which is not the right way to do it. John told me my services were no longer required and I just said 'thanks' and whacked the phone down. He rang back after a while and I told him I thought it was scandalous to think they never called me in to have a chat after all the work I'd done. I told him I felt gutted and my pride had been hurt."

Having arranged to be paid off over a six-month period, Lippiatt finished his conversation with Buchanan and was straight on the phone to Chapple. "To this day he says he knew nothing about it but if I'm honest I'm not 100 per cent convinced," Lippiatt continues. "I instigated him coming back and the directors, who had always backed me, didn't give it enough time for the situation to be turned around. I told Geoff I was staggered the directors hadn't discussed my position with him but he said they didn't. In fairness to him John [Buchanan] did say Geoff knew nothing about it."

Lippiatt grew unhappier as that morning wore on, knowing that Chapple was going to stay put. And in a situation similar to that at Kingstonian when another of Chapple's assistants, Ian McDonald, was removed from his job, Lippiatt thought his partner should have done more. "The bottom line is, if you're a partnership or more like brothers in arms, I would suggest you should have been down to that club wanting to see the board," he maintains. "If it was me I'd have wanted answers as to why it happened and why, as manager, I wasn't consulted. He should have said, 'I'm not having this. Colin brought me back and we've only had a few games together so I want to stick with that partnership to see if it works.' That was the contentious issue for me. The second one is Geoff saying in the press that me going was like a bereavement. I heard on the grapevine from two different people that he was on the phone that afternoon trying to find somebody else to help him. I still feel disappointed we didn't really get to have a go. I feel we still had something to offer and we weren't given long enough."

It was another difficult period in Chapple's life but he adds: "Sometimes it happens in football. I don't think there are any hard feelings now and I think Colin's over it. When there's two of you and one of you goes, naturally that person takes umbrage. But I was talking with Colin about targets on the day he was sacked. It wasn't even on the agenda to sack him apparently. It just came up as loose chat in the board meeting. If I'm lying about it then I've got a bloody good memory haven't I? But Colin doesn't believe that. I certainly never got rid of him. I had nothing to do with his sacking whatsoever. Nothing at all. I've got a clear conscience. But there isn't really a relationship between us now. I could always ring him up but I'm busy on the road and he's busy too at St Albans. We don't speak much now but I remember he told me he wouldn't manage beyond sixty and that was to be his last year. Now he's sixty-five and a few months ago I read somewhere he was going to stay there for another year or two. People change their minds and good luck to him. I follow St Albans now. They're one of the first results I look up, although I don't need to tell Colin that. I'd love to see them go higher."

Chapple is disappointed with how his bond with Lippiatt broke down and adds: "Sometimes when you're that bitter your mind can take over and that's what happened to Colin. He was badmouthing me to a few managers at the time and they were ringing me telling me what he'd said. Ernie Howe at Basingstoke was one and Terry Brown [Aldershot] was another. It was all purely because I was still there at Woking and he wasn't. I could understand his bitterness though. There had been rumblings beforehand about his position and then there were rumblings long before I went too. Insiders had told me to be careful of chairman Chris Ingram not being 100 per cent behind me."

Chapple's time at Woking FC ended in that awful month of September in 2002, when the ejector seat button was pressed barely a year after he had returned. "I had no qualms about leaving Woking in the end," he says. "I couldn't argue with it. We were top of the League in three or four weeks and then fell like a stone in the next three or four."

Chapple insists he tried to do his bit to push Lippiatt into the spotlight a little more over the years but accepts that it was he, as manager, who received most of the recognition. "If I was to sum up our relationship it was that Colin deserves an awful lot of credit for the Chapple years," he says. "I reckon it was fifty-fifty between us. But the manager is always thrust into the limelight and I was aware I had to do things like meet the media. I sometimes let Colin do the press conferences or team talks to be as fair as I could to him. I also tried to get Colin to lead the side out at Wembley one year but that was refused by the FA. Colin was aware of it because I showed him the letter I got back saying it had to be the manager."

Even though he still has misgivings about whether Chapple knew about his sacking from Woking, Lippiatt enjoyed his rise through the non-League ranks at Chapple's side. But, along with Kimber, he knew Chapple better than most and thinks his friend began to believe his own publicity as the years went on. "I personally think Geoff changed over a period of time," he maintains. "I'm not saying he was aware of it, as I've mentioned to him since. But I honestly think, with the greatest respect to him, his halo got too big. He lost sight of the importance of the people around him in terms of their loyalty and integrity. We all know that managers take the spotlight and I admit I found that hard to deal with at times. I was a lot more sensitive back then as everybody knows. But in all the talks he had and stand up presentations over the years, I felt he should have thanked his staff and he didn't. I don't want to bring Barry [Kimber] into it. But we were a trio and on reflection I do feel disappointed Geoff let that side of things slip."

The football side of their relationship never slipped though and Lippiatt eulogises over two of the teams he and Chapple put together when he says: "I can't forget the Windsor team we had back in 1980. Take my word for it they would have been a force in the Conference today. And the Woking 1996/97 team played some unbelievable football, even though towards the end of that season the dressing room wasn't anywhere near as good as it had been. There was whispering behind Geoff's back, no question. It was undermining and there was a lack of respect. One or two players were quite vocal which was disappointing."

One man who knew both Chapple and Lippiatt as if they were his own family was the genial Kimber, the loyal physio who was never tempted to stray from his spiritual home, despite having the chance to go to Kingstonian. He believes football will never see Chapple's like again and he cherishes his time with the man who was one of thirteen managers he worked with at Kingfield. "I didn't have to knock on

Geoff's door, I just went in and sat down," says Kimber. "That's the relationship we had. He left it for me to decide if a player was fit enough and he trusted my decision. There was lots of banter between Geoff, Colin and myself. On away trips, we'd be up playing crib into the early hours for 50p a game and we'd end up fighting over who'd won. Geoff had his style of management and he left Colin to do the coaching. I think he was the most successful non-League manager of all time and Colin was the most successful non-League coach. They didn't get established players in from a higher league. A lot of them came from struggling sides, while the likes of Tim Buzaglo were just local lads. I was privileged to be there during the best time in the history of the club and I'll always have the memories. It's not the same these days. It's no longer a family club, it's just a business. As for Geoff, I don't think anyone will ever win the FA Trophy five times again – let alone in seven years. That is an incredible record that will stand for ever."

As far as Chapple and Lippiatt are concerned, one senses there will always be a feeling of regret felt by both parties at their falling out. And Chapple adds: "I often feel like ringing him up and there's nothing to stop me really. I could never dislike him. We had some great days and we had a lot of fun together."

Lippiatt can't envisage management in football beyond his time at St Albans but despite all that's happened, Chapple has not written off the chances of a comeback with his old pal at some stage. "Who knows, it might happen again," he says. "Funnily enough I haven't ruled it out." A return to the old Clough and Taylor routine maybe? While it is unlikely, only a fool would bet against it.

11

Stars in Their Eyes

'One thing I've learned since becoming a manager is that in the public's mind, players win games and managers lose them' – Bryan Robson

"I was blessed by having good players," he says without the merest hint of hesitation. And therein lies the secret of Geoff Chapple's success. By his own admission, his achievements have come about purely because of the irresistible quality at his disposal out on the pitch. Bringing in that high standard of player, with the help of his assistants – Colin Lippiatt in the main – was his doing of course. But there was little that needed doing to the great teams he built once the pieces were in place other than to let them go out and play.

Having a pass and move philosophy helped. He and Lippiatt both loved to watch it, the players enjoyed producing it and the fans revelled in the beauty of a Chapple team, even though they were certainly capable of under-performing at times; particularly in the bread and butter of the league. Some managers try to stifle talent for the benefit of the team ethos. Chapple let the individual talent flourish. But as well as entertaining, more often than not he had the personnel who also had passion and a will to win, allied to the mental toughness that is the prerequisite for all good footballing sides. There was a potent cocktail in each individual, which made Chapple's teams a cut above the rest.

So how easy is it for him to pick a favourite Woking team, a favourite Kingstonian side and a combined elite capable on their day of winning any Conference championship? Considering the number of players to have graced the two clubs during his tenure as boss, surprisingly easy is the answer. There are contenders in each position naturally. But the names trip off the tongue as readily as goods at the end of a production line, although there was nothing manufactured about a Chapple XI. Rather, it looked the most naturally fitted together of units.

As he was at Woking for around fourteen years, there are a host of contenders for the relevant Cards' jerseys but the goalkeeping one virtually picks itself. "Laurence Batty would be in, no question," says Chapple, his mind ticking over as he launches into his first selection, in what would be a 4-3-1-2 formation. "His all-round game was exceptional and he hardly had any faults," he says. "He had a safe pair of hands, good kicking, wonderful shot-stopping ability and he was experienced too. He was tremendously strong and he would be my keeper."

Right-backs in the frame are Andy Clement and Stewart and John Mitchell, but Chapple goes for a man who was a midfielder by trade. As including him in his team is essential, he is happy to accommodate Shane Wye. "I'd play him at right-back solely to get him in," he says.

Chapple opts for Shane's brother Lloyd at left-back, another easy decision. Such is his admiration for the pair, the boss had even paid their airfares back from New Zealand in the early Conference years after they had moved to the southern hemisphere to play for Wanganui Athletic. "Those two only knew one thing and that was to win," he says. "If they lost they lost with blood on them but for the right reasons."

No surprises too at the first player named as centre-back. "In that position the first name on the team-sheet would be Kevan Brown," he says. "I brought him in to the club and he didn't do particularly well at first, playing at right-back. Then he walked into my office one day and said, 'I can play at centre-back.' I thought about it and we tried it out. It was the best thing he ever said to me. Like I say he didn't set the world alight when he first came, but he was superb in the centre and was a tremendous performer. He was a good captain and tremendously reliable. Apart from that he was also a thoroughly decent bloke."

While there are several candidates for the left-sided centre-back berth, Chapple chooses a man who had come with him through the ranks at Windsor, a natural left-sided player whose inclusion gives a nice balance. "I'd probably have to go for Trevor Baron," he says. "He was another thoroughly nice chap and one of life's gentlemen. He was left sided, strong in the air and the one good thing about Trevor was that if we were ever in trouble and were losing, he'd get up the other end and score for us. He was a Rolls Royce of a defender. I could also have had Mark Tucker or Steve Foster. Steve was someone who, when I first saw him, I knew was going to be a hell of a player. We paid £9,000 for him from Telford and sold him for £150,000 to Bristol Rovers, which wasn't bad business. It's a toss of a coin between Trevor and Steve but I'd go for Trevor on the basis he was with me a lot longer. In the modern day game, Fossie would have the nod though."

Unlucky to be left out, purely because of the system not being 5-3-2, is Adie Cowler, another inspirational skipper and driving force in Woking's rise to the Conference. Gwynne Berry and Colin Fielder were mentioned too, with Chapple adding: "Gwynne was strong while Colin was one of the best signings I ever made for Woking. We swapped him for George Friel who went to Slough. It was a bit of a gamble bringing Colin in, although I knew him from his Aldershot days and he turned out to be a magnificent signing."

To the midfield then, and Chapple warms to his task, loving every minute as he reels off the names as the memories come flooding back. "I cannot leave Steve Thompson out, for his engine – he never ran out of gas and was absolutely magnificent – and I cannot leave Mark Biggins out for sheer entertainment, creativity and tricks on the ball," he says adamantly. Making up the trio in midfield alongside those two is Dereck Brown, another who was one of life's good guys. "Thommo and Dereck would be up and down while Biggo would be getting on too," says Chapple with gusto, appearing not to worry about who would take on defensive duties. The one behind the front two doesn't take too much working out either; Scott Steele's impish skills terrorised the best Conference defences when he was given licence to run at the opposition.

That leaves the two front runners. "There are two in particular who are first on the sheet," says Chapple. "The rest of the contenders couldn't even lace their boots," he says. "Tim Buzaglo and Clive Walker would walk in. Clive and Scottie were telepathic and Tim was an exceptional goalscorer. Tim and Clive never got to play together but they would have scored a goal or two. That team would have got goals from the back as well as up front. In my original selection I had Jody Craddock [who later played in the Premiership with Sunderland] at centre-back, but he wasn't with us long enough. He was only on loan, but in terms of a player he'd be in there. He was only a young lad at the time but he did ever so well. So did Tim Alexander. He changed Woking's season on his own one year. He made his debut at Merthyr Tydfil and never looked back. Andy Parr was a good penalty taker, striker George Friel was a great signing and scored hatfuls of goals for us while Paul Mulvaney was another good forward."

Just for good measure Chapple names five substitutes in his Woking team, opting not to do so later on for the Kingstonian version in view of the lesser amount of time he spent at Kingsmeadow. First in is soldier Chris 'Spider' Lomas, a Card in the mid-1980s, as his substitute goalkeeper. "He was not the biggest but he was reliable and a bloody good keeper," says the boss. "For a defender I'll have Mark Tucker and I'll have two midfielders, both of them Andy's, Ellis and Parr. For the last place I'll go for a striker in Darran Hay, with George Friel close behind."

Interestingly, Chapple's assistant for much of his Woking career, Lippiatt, has a slightly different side although he too opts for 4-3-1-2. And while the positives on each player were numerous, Lippiatt is happy to throw in a negative or two for each of his selections, Batty being the first. "Laurence was the best I've seen, he had everything although he could get sucked in on his near post," says Lippiatt. "The only frailty he had was he was a bit negative in his own mind about injuries. He was a bit of a baby I thought."

Stewart Mitchell, Tucker, Baron and Lloyd Wye are his back four, Mitchell and Tucker the two differences from Chapple's team. "Stewart was the best right-back I saw at Woking, a thin, wiry looking lad but tenacious in the tackle. He was a very consistent performer. Lloyd was a total winner who gave you 100 per cent plus and never really had a bad game. He could be accused of being a one-peg player. But he was a good left-back. Trevor was the Rolls Royce and a very cultured player. He sometimes overplayed and gambled at times, which can catch you out defensively. But he was capable of getting you a goal too. I liked Tucker. The criticism was in his make up for me. He was a moody player and a moody person but as a defender he was strong in the air, decent on the deck and attacked the ball quickly."

On to the midfield players and Lippiatt also opts for Biggins, Brown and Thompson; but Biggins is the man in the hole behind the front two for Lippiatt, while Shane Wye commands the third middle-of-the-park slot. "Dereck was the best midfield player I would say," he continues. "You won't find many better box-to-box players and he could attack and get at people. Biggins had it in his locker to change a game and destroy the opposition. Sometimes he wasn't quite mentally right and he couldn't deal with being man-marked. Thommo had a much better make-up mentally and he was unbelievably fit, while I always liked Shane. He could be moody and had a few rows with people but he was a great passer who showed great use of the ball and was a great tackler."

Lippiatt needs no prompting to pick out his two front men. Like Chapple, he doesn't look beyond Walker and Buzaglo and says: "I never liked Clive Walker and nor did Geoff. I wouldn't trust him as far as I could throw him. But I got him down at Woking after first telling Geoff I didn't think he could do it. And what I would say is nobody could ever deny the contribution he made. Because of his background he milked that a bit. Other players in the team didn't get the just rewards or the media attention they deserved because, I don't care what anybody says, it's not about one player. Yes, Clive was a significant signing and made a big difference to us, but he wasn't always the best player away from home and I've seen him at places like Altrincham and Macclesfield where his contribution was very little."

Buzaglo made a huge impression on anyone who saw him play, not least Lippiatt. "I would say he was one of the top three strikers I've ever seen. He had everything. He was wrongly accused of being lazy, although he could be ineffective at times and he lacked drive and ambition. It was one of the funniest things I ever saw when he fell asleep in the dugout before a game at Kidderminster. But at the end of the day strikers are there to score goals and affect play in the final third. That's what Tim did. When he got spinning people and turning he was absolute quality and a joy to watch."

While both Chapple and Lippiatt's Woking teams would have given any side in the Conference a game they would remember, Chapple's Kingstonian team too, also a 4-3-1-2 formation, would have been equally dynamic. Steve Farrelly takes Chapple's goalkeeping slot. "That's easy," he says. "Steve was another with a massive presence. He was susceptible to one or two little errors mainly because his legs were so long, but he was another great keeper. I remember he played out of his skin at Brentford in the FA Cup. He didn't have a lot to do but what he did do, he did fantastically well. He complained of neck pains after the game but no-one thought it was a serious problem. I got a call the next day from the Royal Surrey Hospital in Guildford. They didn't know what was wrong with him but he was boiling hot one minute and shivering the next. His temperature was sky high and after a few days they gave him an

MRI scan and found he had a blood clot which could have killed him. He did recover thankfully."

At right-back Tarkan Mustafa gets the Chapple vote, the elegant defender with attacking flair having been picked up from Barnet reserves. "When I first saw him I thought 'he can play'. He's not the best defensively but he could change defence into attack in seconds."

At left-back Colin Luckett is the chosen one. "Colin was not the quickest but was a good defender, with a tremendous left foot who could score goals," adds Chapple. "He was good in the air too and had an all-round game. Both Tarkan and Colin were regulars right the way through my time at Kingstonian."

Another 'Captain Fantastic' takes the first of the central defensive slots. Matt Crossley, a star at Wycombe Wanderers prior to his arrival at Kingsmeadow, was due to join Chapple at Woking in 1997 before the boss realised he was on his way to rivals Ks. "Matt was elegant, a Trevor Baron type," he says. "He was very cool under pressure. I had some good centre halves in Mark Harris and Wayne Brown but I have gone for Terry Evans alongside Matt. Terry was a man-mountain. He only had a season with us but was a massive presence."

In midfield Chapple was blessed with two of the finest operators ever to have graced the non-League game and it comes as no surprise they are in his team. Pitcher and Patterson flowed off the tongue and the two of them, Geoff and Gary, dovetailed into an exciting combination in the heart of the team. Chapple has gone for Pitcher in the hole behind the front two though, with Patterson joined in a midfield three by Kevin Rattray and Phil Wingfield.

Rattray was with Chapple at Woking, having been picked up from parks football. Wingfield provided a constant source of ammunition for the strikers with his penetrating left foot. "Up front I would have liked to include a loan player," says Chapple. "Lee Boylan came in for me twice from West Ham on loan and I had a young lad named Ronnie Green who threatened to do well for me. Then there was Gavin Holligan who wasn't with me long enough because Harry [Redknapp] nicked him for West Ham. But the two I've gone for in attack are Dave Leworthy, obviously, and Eddie Akuamoah. Eddie was quick and skilful while Dave had great awareness. He'd score goals when nobody would expect him too. He always knew where the goalkeeper was. If he was on the halfway line he'd know and the amount of times I saw him put a ball over the keeper's head from forty yards was incredible. He had a great touch and would have been with me a lot longer if I'd got him at Woking. Dave wanted to come to Kingfield but I couldn't afford him. In the end he went down to Dover to play for them. He got hat-tricks galore."

So there they are. Chapple's two teams and Lippiatt's Woking side for good measure. How they would have fared against each other one can only speculate, but all three would have caressed the ball around the park and created openings against the most stubborn of outfits. These days the professional era has given way to percentage football. But as any Woking or Kingstonian fan will tell you, the nearest a Chapple team came to knocking the ball in the channel was when they were away at Dover.

Chapple's all time XI, a mixture from both Woking and Kingstonian, is a 4-3-3 formation and reads, Batty, Mustafa, Crossley, Brown, Luckett, Thompson, Pitcher, Patterson, Walker, Buzaglo, Leworthy. So how would Chapple have enjoyed leading that collection of gems? "It would have been a piece of cake," he says. "It would have been poetry in motion. The second XI would have been just as good, pretty near. For example you'd never leave out the Wye brothers in a second team, nor Trevor Baron. When you think of the pleasure I've had watching some of those players play; well, it's been fantastic."

Fantastic too for the supporters who, from the late 1980s, began flocking in their ever-increasing numbers to see football played in the way it was intended, thanks to one man's philosophy – an ideal that was expressed through the coaches who shared his beliefs. Some he has worked with have less than fond memories of Chapple, but then over a twenty-five-year spell a football manager would expect to put a few noses out of joint along the way. It goes with the territory. Even so, the majority of those who have been touched in some way by Chapple's own brand of magic have gone with the flow and enjoyed the moment. For them those times will always be fondly remembered, while future non-League historians will always revere his record. Some may even question whether his Wembley exploits could possibly have happened. They did.

And in those quiet moments, when Geoff Chapple has slumped down on his settee at home in Farnham after another day dropping off parcels to all corners of the UK, he can feel a certain satisfaction at a good job done. It is a similar feeling, albeit on a lesser scale, to the warm glow that washes over him when recalling his life in football. After all there is a common theme. He delivered.

Geoff Chapple's Managerial Achievements

Alton Town

(player-manager season 1978/79)

1978/79: Athenian League Cup winners.

Windsor & Eton

(August 1981 to September 1984)

1982/83: Isthmian League Division Two runners-up (promotion to First Division);
FA Cup first round lost to Brentford.
1983/84: Isthmian League Division One champions (promotion to Premier Division);
FA Cup second round replay lost to Bournemouth.

Woking

(September 1984 to May 1997, and October 2001 to October 2002)

1986/87: Isthmian League Division Two South champions.
1988/89: FA Cup first round lost to Cambridge United.
1989/90: Isthmian League Division One runners-up; FA Cup second round lost to Cambridge United.
1990/91: FA Cup third round beat West Bromwich Albion; FA Cup fourth round lost to Everton; Surrey Senior Cup winners; AC Delco Isthmian League Cup winners.

1991/92: Isthmian League Premier Division champions (promotion to Conference); Isthmian League Charity Shield winners; FA Cup third round replay lost to Hereford United.

1992/93: Isthmian League Charity Shield winners; FA Cup second round replay lost to Brighton & Hove Albion.

1993/94: Third in Conference; FA Trophy winners; Surrey Senior Cup winners.

1994/95: Conference runners-up; FA Trophy winners; APL Championship Shield winners; FA Cup second round lost to Marlow.

1995/96: Conference runners-up; FA Cup third round lost to Swindon Town; Surrey Senior Cup winners.

1996/97: FA Trophy winners; FA Cup third round replay lost to Coventry City, having beaten Millwall and Cambridge United in first and second rounds respectively.

Kingstonian

(August 1997 to May 2001)

1997/98: Isthmian League Premier Division champions (promotion to Conference); Surrey Senior Cup winners; Isthmian League Charity Shield winners.

1998/99: FA Trophy winners; Conference Charity Shield winners; FA Cup second round replay lost to Leyton Orient.

1999/00: FA Trophy winners; Conference League Cup finalists; Conference Charity Shield finalists; FA Cup first round lost to Luton Town.

2000/01: FA Cup fourth round replay lost to Bristol City having beaten Brentford and Southend United in first and third rounds respectively.

If you are interested in purchasing other books published by Stadia, or in case you have difficulty finding any Stadia books in your local bookshop, you can also place orders directly through the Tempus Publishing website

www.tempus-publishing.com